Fashion Design Sketchbook

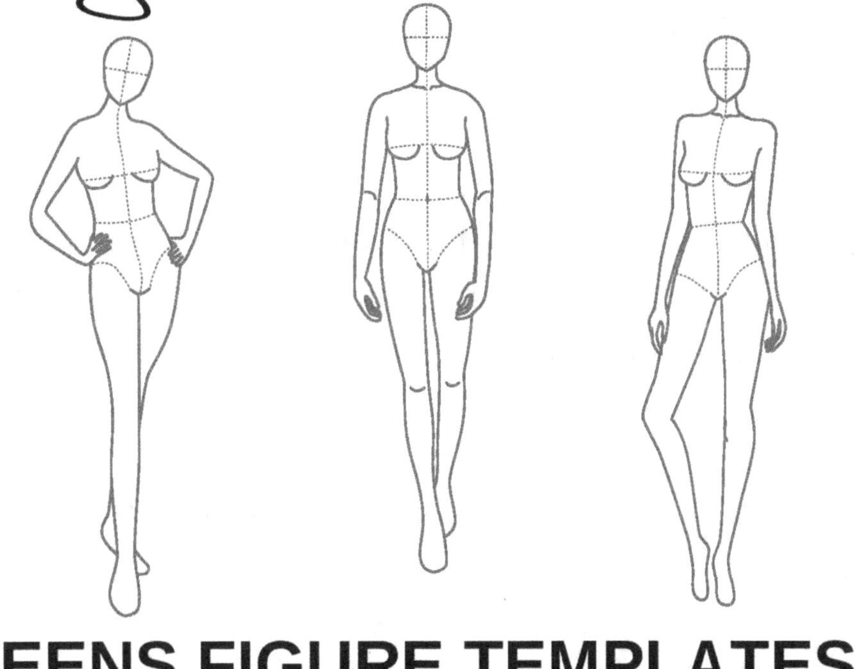

TEENS FIGURE TEMPLATES

From Beginner to Advanced

Niky Jadesson

© Copyright 2025 – Niky Jadesson
All rights reserved.

No part of this book may be reproduced, stored in a retrieval system, or transmitted in any form or by any means – electronic, mechanical, photocopying, recording, or otherwise – without prior written permission of the author or publisher.

Legal Notice:
This publication is protected by copyright law. It is intended for personal, educational, and non-commercial use only. Copying, modifying, selling, or distributing any portion of this book without written consent is strictly prohibited.

Disclaimer:
This sketchbook is created for educational and creative learning purposes. While every effort has been made to provide accurate and inspiring material, the author and publisher make no guarantees regarding results or outcomes. The content is designed for students and young creatives interested in fashion illustration and design practice.
The author and publisher disclaim any liability arising from the use of this book.

Thank you for respecting the rights of the creator!

Dedication Page

To every young dreamer who believes that fashion is an art of self-expression,

This book was made for you - to explore, to practice, and to create with confidence.

Let each page remind you that your imagination is powerful and your ideas matter.

Keep sketching, keep dreaming, and never stop believing in your unique style.

With creativity and heart,

Niky Jadesson

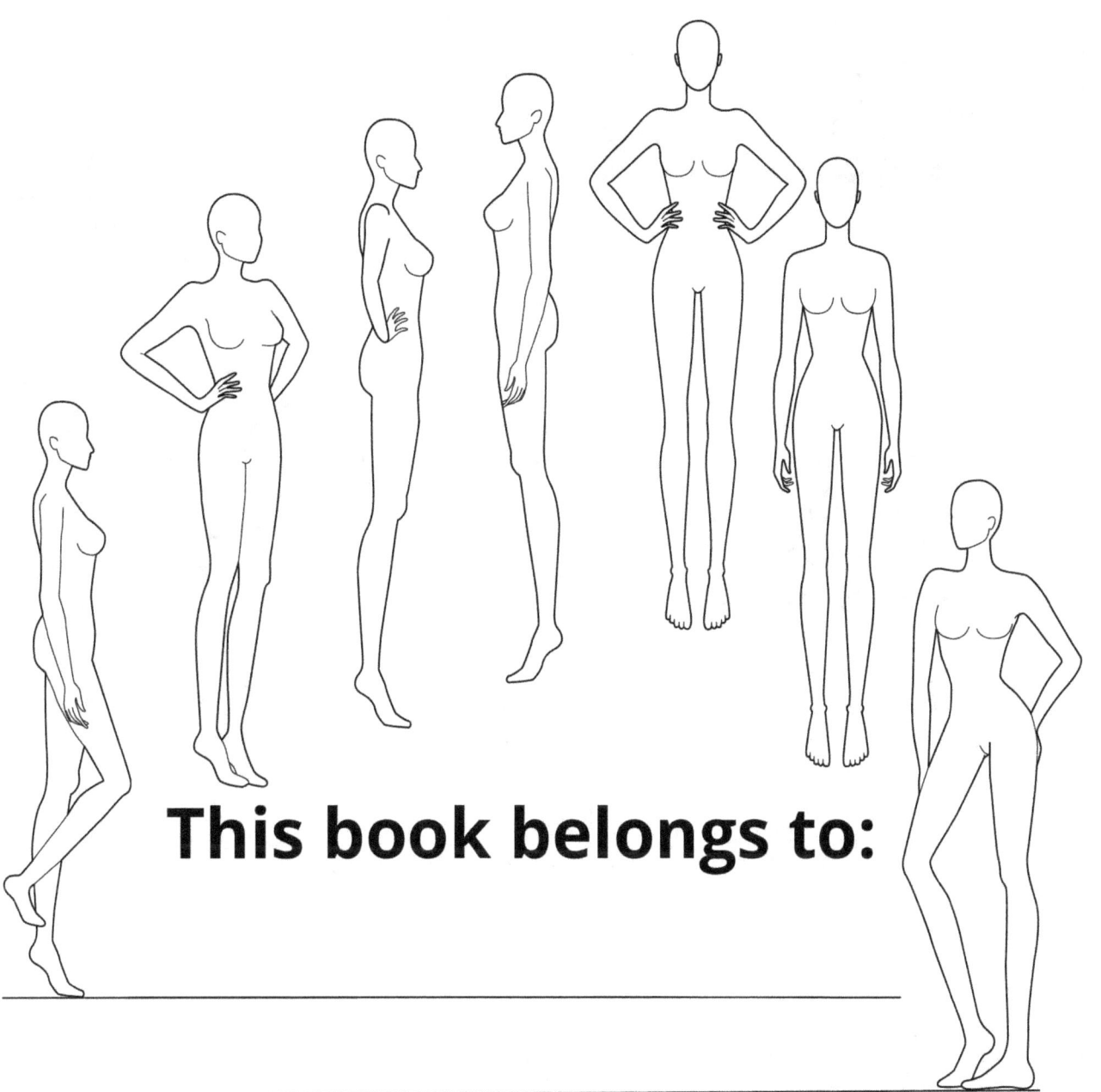

This book belongs to:

_____
(your name)

Niky Jadesson

Dear Young Designer,

Thank you for choosing this sketchbook and for starting your creative journey!

I hope it inspires you to explore fashion, sketch boldly, and have fun learning new ideas. Each page is your space to experiment, practice, and express your personal style.

If you'd like to stay updated on future books or share your feedback, I'd love to hear from you.
Just search for **"Niky Jadesson Books"** online.

Your support means the world. If this book brings value to you, leaving a short review helps other readers discover it and supports independent publishing.

With gratitude,

★ ★ ★ ★ ★

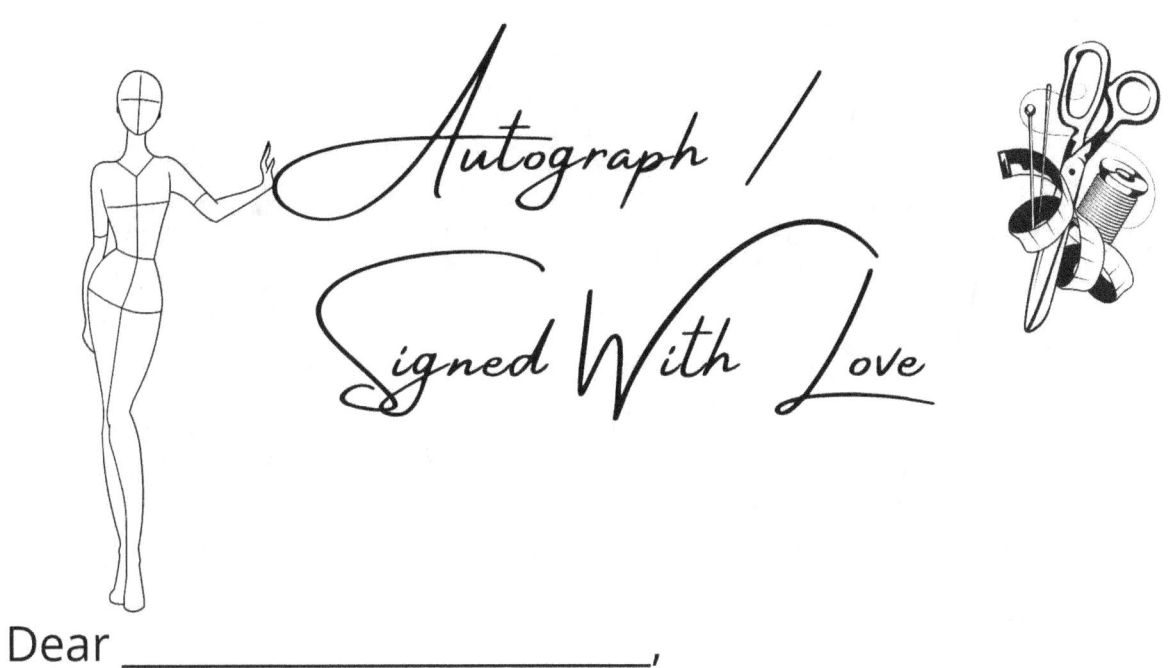

Autograph / Signed With Love

Dear _____,

This sketchbook is for you - to design, to imagine, and to express your unique vision.

Remember: every line you draw brings you one step closer to becoming a real fashion designer.

With all my heart,

_____
(Signature)

Date: _____

Table of Contents

Part I – Intro Pages

1. Title Page 1
2. Copyright Page.. 2
3. Dedication Page 3
4. Coloring Pages (Creative Inserts) 4, 6, 8, 10, 14, 16, 34, 144, 146
5. This book belongs to 5
6. Thank You! (Intro Message) 7
7. Autograph / Signed With Love 9
8. Table of Contents 11-12
9. Welcome! 13
10. Author's Preface 15
11. How to Use This Sketchbook 17
12. My Goals & Inspirations 18
13. Tools & Materials for Teen Fashion Sketching.....................................19
14. Tips for Getting Started.. 20

Part II – Education & Fundamentals 21

15. A Short History of Teen Fashion – From Classic Styles to Modern Vibes 22
16. Teen Silhouettes & Body Shapes – Finding Your Style 23
17. Color Theory in Teen Fashion – Express Yourself! 24
18. Fabrics & Textures – How Clothes Come to Life 25
19. Fashion Sketching Tools – Traditional & Digital 26
20. Step-by-Step: Casual Day Outfit (Everyday Style) 27
21. Step-by-Step: Party or Evening Look 28
22. Common Design Mistakes (and How to Avoid Them) 29
23. Tips & Tricks for Teen Designers 30
24. Step-by-Step Guide to This Sketchbook 31
25. Fashion Sketching Fundamentals - Step by Step 32
26. Quick & Easy Everyday Fashion Look 33

Table of Contents

Part III – Sketchbook & Practice 35

27. Fashion Practice Guide & Notes... 36, 44, 51, 58, 65, 72, 80, 87, 94, 101, 108, 116

28. Outfit Inspiration: Streetwear 37, 45, 52, 59, 66, 73, 81, 88, 95, 102, 109, 117

29. Body Templates – Teen Silhouettes (Front, Back, Side Views) 38–41, 46-48, 53-55, 60-62, 67-69, 74-77, 82-84, 89-91, 96-98, 103-105, 110-113, 118-120, 123-130

30. Your Notes & Inspiration Photos 42, 49, 56, 63, 70, 78, 85, 92, 99, 106, 114, 121

31. Outfit Inspiration: School, Weekend & Trend Looks 43, 50, 57, 64, 71, 79, 86, 93, 100, 107, 115, 122

⭐ *Note*: *The Body Templates – Teen Silhouettes and practice pages are intentionally repeated to encourage confidence, creativity, and consistent style development.*

Part IV – Closing & Extras 131

32. Body Templates – Teen Silhouettes (Front, Back, Side Views) 132
33. Creative Exercises 133-140
34. Designer Checklist for Teens 141
35. My Favorite Fabrics & Brands – Notes & Swatches 142
36. My Personal Fashion Journal 143
37. Congratulations! You Did It! 145
38. Thank You! (final message) 147
39. Thank You for Choosing This Book! 148
40. About the Author 149
41. Mini Glossary of Fashion Terms (for Teens) 150
42. Certificate of Completion Fashion Design Sketchbook – Teen Edition 151

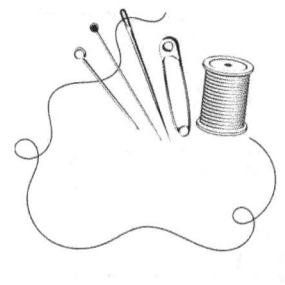  

Hey there, creative soul - welcome to your fashion world!

Fashion isn't just about clothes or trends - it's about you. It's how you express who you are, what inspires you, and the confidence you carry.

Each sketch you draw tells a story, and every design you imagine brings your personality to life.

This sketchbook was created to help you explore, experiment, and grow as a young designer.

Take your time, play with shapes, fabrics, and colors - and most of all, enjoy the process!

Whether you're a beginner just starting out, or already building your own style, this is your safe space to dream big and sketch freely.

We're so excited to be part of your creative journey.
Now grab your pencil - your fashion story starts here!

Happy designing,

Niky Jadesson

Author's Preface

Dear Reader,

Welcome to the teen edition of the Fashion Design Sketchbook!

This book was created to inspire your imagination and guide your creativity - whether you dream of becoming a designer or simply love expressing yourself through art.

Inside, you'll find both structure and freedom:
- Structure - pages that teach you about silhouettes, fabrics, and sketching techniques.
- Freedom - templates, outfit ideas, and creative exercises that let your personality shine.

Fashion is about confidence - it's your voice without words.

Through every sketch, I hope you'll learn to trust your style and discover what makes your vision unique.

So don't worry about "perfect" lines. What matters most is that you keep creating, keep exploring, and keep having fun.

With passion and gratitude,
Niky Jadesson

How to Use This Sketchbook

This sketchbook is your creative playground - a mix of learning, practicing, and dreaming!

Here's how to get the most out of it:

- **Experiment Freely** – Try out different outfit ideas, silhouettes, and colors. Don't be afraid to make mistakes - they're part of learning.
- **Take Notes** – Write down your ideas, trends you love, or fabrics that inspire you.
- **Use the Templates** – The teen body figures help you visualize real proportions and design balanced outfits.
- **Add Inspiration** – Paste magazine cutouts, photos, or fabric swatches in the notes pages.
- **Compare & Improve** – Redraw older designs to see how much you've grown.
- **Build Collections** – Try designing themed outfits (streetwear, school looks, partywear).

Whether you're sketching for fun or planning your fashion future, this book is your studio - a place where creativity and confidence come together.

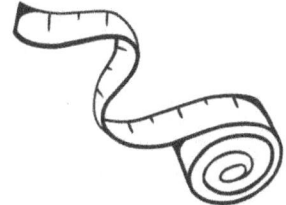

My Goals & Inspirations

Fashion design is more than drawing clothes - it's about expressing your mood, lifestyle, and imagination.

Use this page to reflect on what inspires you most and where you want your creativity to go.

Ask yourself:
- What kind of fashion do I love most? (streetwear, party looks, Y2K, minimal, sporty-chic)
- Who inspires me? (designers, influencers, artists, or even friends)
- What emotions do I want my clothes to express? (confidence, joy, power, freedom)

Write it down here:
- My design goals: ....
- My biggest inspirations: ....
- Fabrics or colors I want to explore: ....
- Skills I want to improve: ....

Tip: *Revisit this page every few months - you'll be amazed at how your vision evolves as you grow.*

Tools & Materials
for Teen Fashion Sketching

You don't need fancy or expensive tools to be creative - just curiosity and a few essentials!

- **Pencils** – Use HB for outlines, 2B–6B for shading details and folds.
- **Fineliners** – For sharp outlines or fun doodle details.
- **Markers & Colored Pencils** – Bring your designs to life with color and texture. Try blending pastels or neon accents for trend looks!
- **Ruler & Curves** – Great for skirts, jackets, and sharp details.
- **Digital Tools** – If you love tech, try drawing apps like Procreate or Sketchbook.
- **Fabric Swatches** – Touching real materials helps you imagine how your design will move.

Remember: The magic isn't in the tool - it's in how you use it to tell your story.

Tips
for Getting Started

Starting something new can feel intimidating - but every great designer began with a blank page!

Here are a few tips to help you start strong:
- **Keep It Simple** – Begin with easy pieces like tops, jeans, or dresses.
- **Observe & Learn** – Look at how real clothes fit, fold, and move.
- **Play with Shapes** – Try different silhouettes: oversized, cropped, flared, fitted.
- **Experiment with Color** – Mix shades that represent your vibe - soft pastels, cool tones, or bold brights.
- **Stay Confident** – Don't worry about "perfect" drawings. Your style will evolve with every page.

Every sketch is progress - every mistake teaches you something new.
The more you draw, the more you shine through your designs.

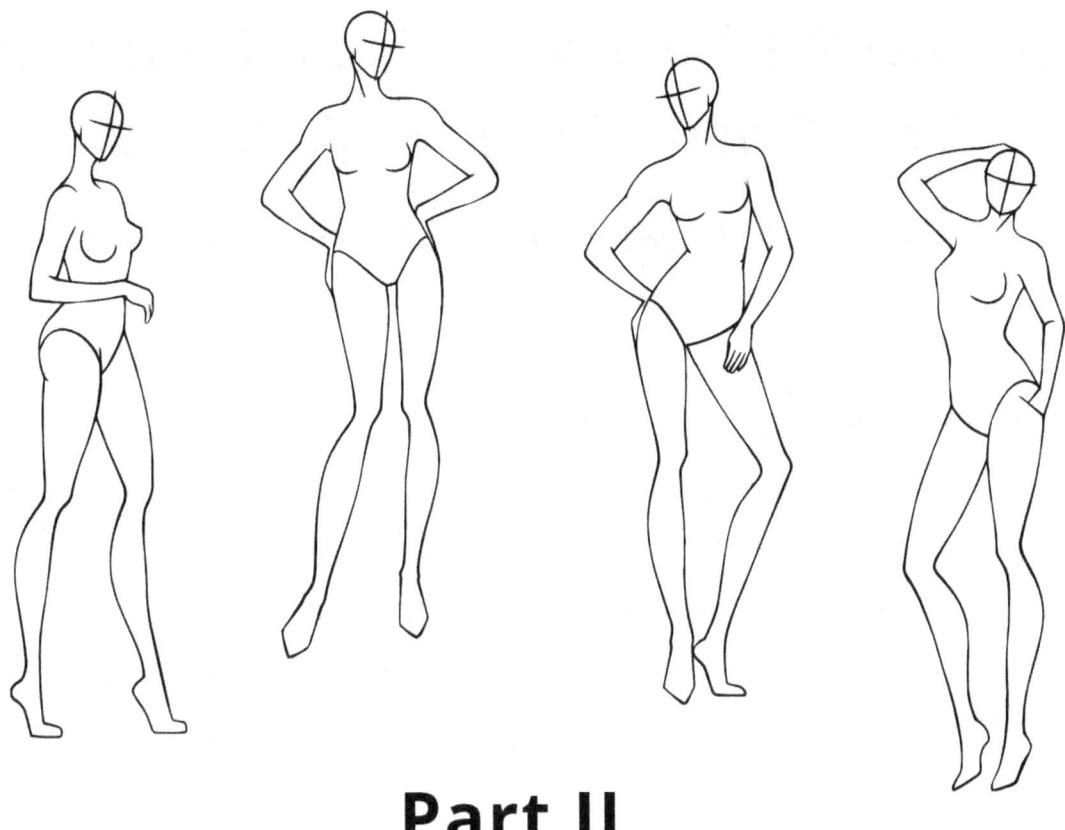

Part II
– Education & Fundamentals

This section introduces the basics of fashion design - the building blocks that help every idea take shape.

Here you'll discover how fashion evolved, how silhouettes and fabrics create moods, and how color can change everything about a design.

Read, learn, and most importantly - apply it when you start sketching your own outfits.

A Short History of Teen Fashion
– *From Classic Styles to Modern Vibes*

Fashion for teens has always been about freedom, creativity, and identity. Every generation has reinvented what it means to be "stylish."

- **1950s – Retro Beginnings**

Circle skirts, cardigans, and neat hairstyles were popular. Teenagers started influencing fashion for the first time!

- **1970s–1980s – The Rebellion Years**

Rock, punk, and disco styles exploded. Teens mixed leather jackets, denim, and bold prints - fashion became a form of protest and fun.

- **1990s–2000s – Cool & Casual**

Streetwear took over: baggy jeans, crop tops, hoodies, and sneakers. Comfort met attitude.

- **Today – Creative Freedom**

Modern teen fashion blends everything: vintage pieces, gender-neutral looks, oversized fits, Y2K inspiration, and eco-friendly choices.

The best part? There are no strict rules anymore - fashion is about being you.

Teen Silhouettes & Body Shapes
– Finding Your Style

Every outfit starts with a silhouette - the shape that defines your design's mood and movement.

- **Relaxed Fit** – Loose, casual, comfy. Great for hoodies, tees, and streetwear.
- **Fitted** – Highlights the body's natural shape. Perfect for dresses or tailored jackets.
- **A-Line** – Slightly flared; fun and flattering for skirts and dresses.
- **Layered** – Combines oversized tops with fitted bottoms (or vice versa). Adds personality!

Tip: *Don't stress about "perfect" proportions - use them as a guide. What matters is how your design feels.*

Color Theory in Teen Fashion
– Express Yourself!

Color makes a design pop and tells the world who you are before you say a word.

- **Warm vs. Cool Tones**

Warm colors (reds, yellows, corals) = energy and fun.
Cool tones (blues, greens, purples) = calm and confidence.

- **Contrast & Balance**

Opposites attract! Try pairing black & white, or pink & teal for bold effects.
Soft blends (pastels or neutrals) give a calm, aesthetic vibe.

- **Seasonal Inspiration**
    - *Spring*: pastels & light shades
    - *Summer*: bright, beachy tones
    - *Autumn*: earthy, cozy hues
    - *Winter*: dark contrasts & sparkle
- **Your Style Palette**

Think of colors that feel like you. Mix, test, and find your signature vibe!

Fabrics & Textures
– *How Clothes Come to Life*

Fabric changes everything about how a design feels and moves.

- **Cotton & Jersey** – Soft, breathable, and great for everyday looks.
- **Denim** – Timeless and tough. From jackets to jeans, it never goes out of style.
- **Satin & Silk** – Shiny, elegant, perfect for formal or glam outfits.
- **Knits & Fleece** – Cozy textures for casual or sporty pieces.
- **Leather & Faux Leather** – Adds edge and attitude to your look.

Exercise: *Sketch the same outfit twice - once in denim, once in satin. Notice how the whole mood changes!*

Fashion Sketching Tools
– *Traditional & Digital*

The right tools make sketching fun and help you bring ideas to life.

- **Pencils** – Perfect for quick outlines and shading.
- **Markers** – Use them for color experiments and trendy highlights.
- **Colored Pencils** – Great for adding soft tones or gradients.
- **Fineliners** – Define shapes, patterns, or outlines.
- **Watercolors** – Add movement and artistic flair.
- **Digital Tools** – Drawing tablets or apps (like Procreate or Ibis Paint) let you test endless colors and undo mistakes easily!

Remember*: Don't wait for perfect tools - start with what you have. Creativity > equipment.*

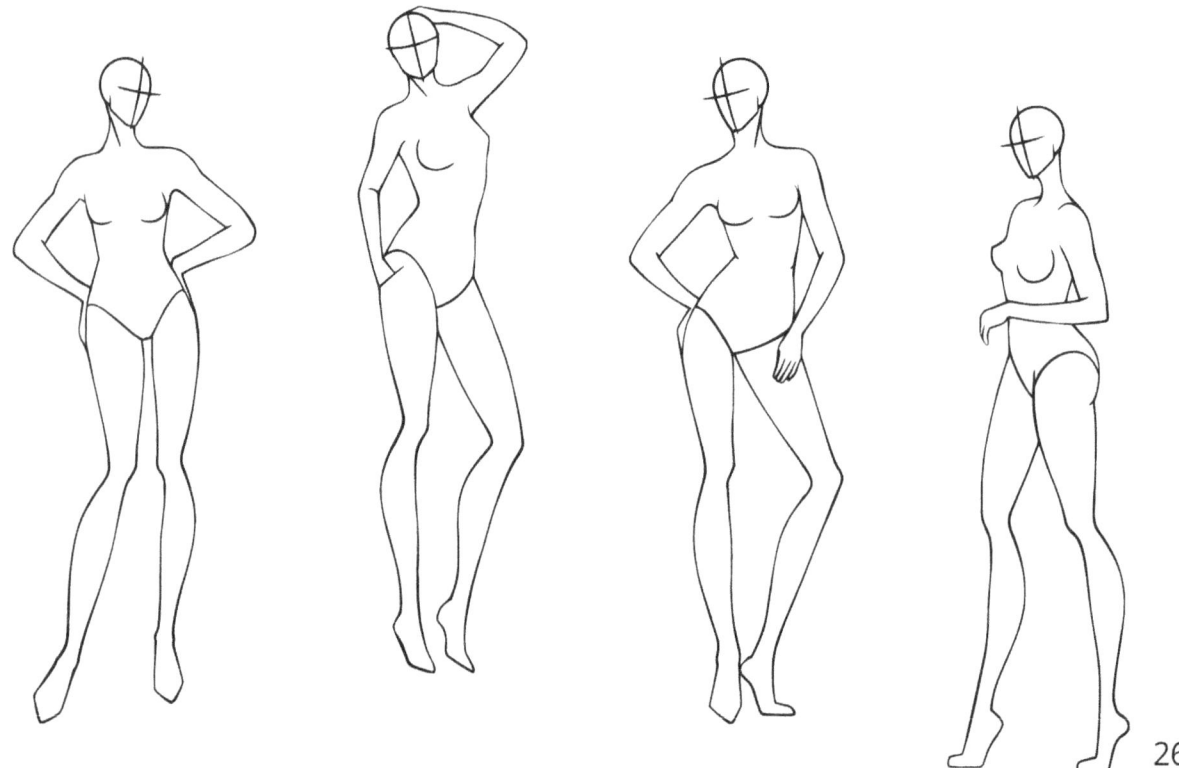

Step-by-Step:
Casual Day Outfit (Everyday Style)

Everyday fashion = comfort + personality.

Here's how to design your first casual outfit:
1. **Start with the base silhouette.** Choose a relaxed or slightly fitted figure.
2. **Add the outfit pieces.** Try a t-shirt, cropped top, or hoodie.
3. **Choose bottoms.** Jeans, shorts, or a flowy skirt.
4. **Add accessories.** Think backpacks, sneakers, or layered jewelry.
5. **Play with colors.** Try mixing neutrals with one standout shade.

Pro Tip: *A great casual design looks effortless but feels confident.*

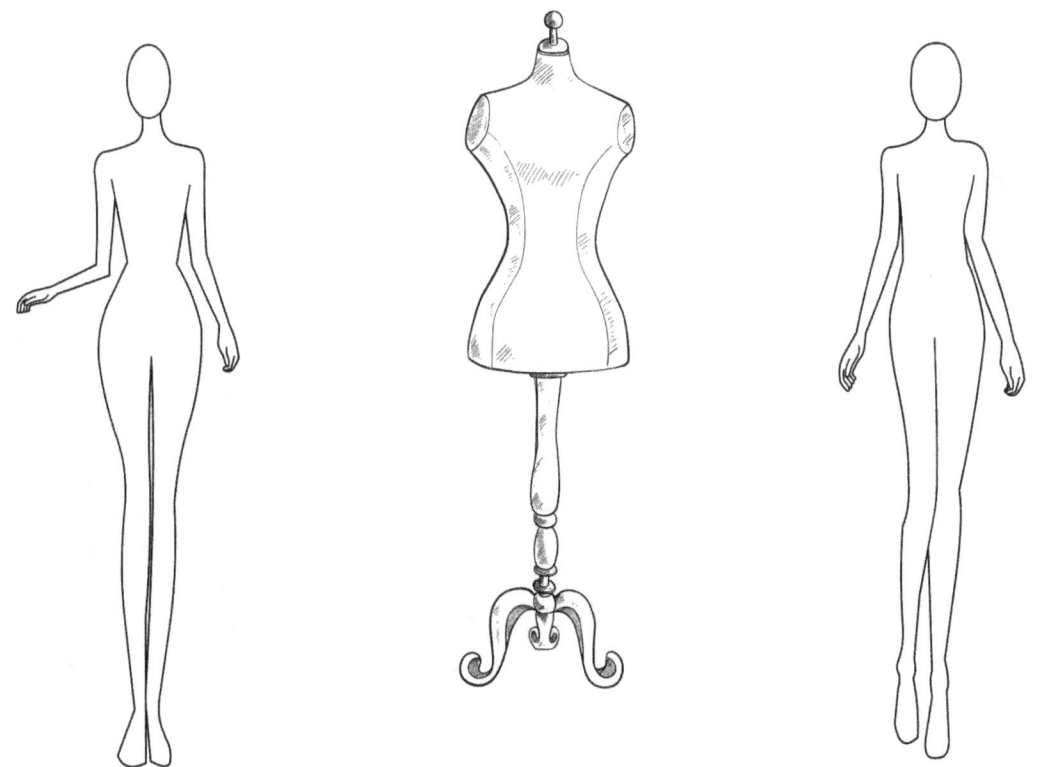

Step-by-Step:
Party or Evening Look

It's time to shine!

Designing partywear is about expressing confidence and creativity.

1. **Pick a silhouette.** Fitted, flared, or flowy?
2. **Choose fabrics.** Satin, sequins, tulle - anything that stands out.
3. **Add statement details.** Ruffles, sparkles, off-shoulder cuts, or bold sleeves.
4. **Select colors.** Metallics, jewel tones, or deep shades look amazing.
5. **Add the final touch.** Accessories like heels, bags, or chokers complete the look.

Your goal: *make the outfit feel special - something that celebrates your vibe.*

Common Design Mistakes
(and How to Avoid Them)

Even pros make these - so learn early and skip the frustration!

- **Too Many Details** – Simplicity often wins. Pick one focus point.
- **Ignoring Movement** – Always imagine how the fabric will flow when worn.
- **Color Overload** – Balance bold colors with neutral tones.
- **Proportion Mix-Ups** – Keep top and bottom shapes balanced.
- **Copying Trends Blindly** – Use inspiration, but add your own twist.

Remember: *Every mistake is a creative lesson - it helps you grow faster.*

Tips & Tricks
for Teen Designers

- Draw many versions of the same idea - that's how real collections are born.
- Try mix-and-match outfits. Make every piece reusable in new looks.
- Keep a small "fashion moodboard" - photos, quotes, fabric scraps, colors.
- Study proportions and fabric flow - clothes should move.
- Don't compare your style - develop your own aesthetic step by step.

Design isn't about being perfect. It's about telling a story through clothes.

Step-by-Step Guide
to This Sketchbook

This sketchbook is more than blank pages - it's your creative diary.

Here's how to use it best:
- **Practice**: Start with the templates. Focus on confidence, not perfection.
- **Experiment**: Try color palettes, fabrics, and textures you've never used before.
- **Document**: Use note pages for reflections or to paste inspirations.
- **Build Collections**: Create themed outfits - back-to-school, streetwear, formal, etc.
- **Review**: Compare old and new sketches to see your progress.

By the last page, you'll have not just designs - but your personal fashion evolution.

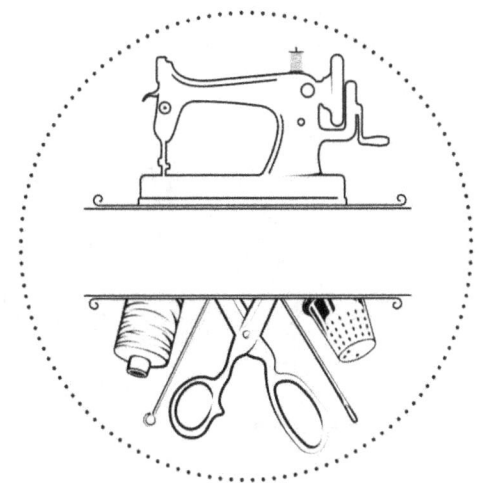

Fashion Sketching Fundamentals
- *Step by Step*

Learning how to sketch fashion is all about practice. Follow this simple process:

Step 1:
- Draw a light outline of the teen body silhouette (front view).

Step 2:
- Add basic garment shapes (hoodie, skirt, pants, dress).

Step 3:
- Include details - seams, buttons, collars, patterns.

Step 4:
- Use linework to show fabric type (soft or structured).

Step 5:
- Add shading and color.

Step 6:
- Outline final lines and make notes.

Mini Challenge:
Draw one outfit for a "chill weekend" and one for a "special event." See how small changes (color, texture) totally change the mood!

QUICK & EASY EVERYDAY FASHION LOOK

Let's put it all into practice!

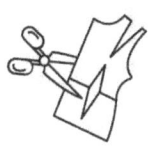

5 Simple Steps:
1. Draw a casual figure pose.
2. Add comfy clothes - t-shirt, jeans, or hoodie.
3. Include a few accessories - bag, shoes, jewelry.
4. Pick your color palette (try neutrals + one bright accent).
5. Add shadows and textures to bring it to life.

Style Note: Everyday looks are the best way to practice proportion, movement, and balance.

Reflection Prompt:
- What outfit would you wear every day if you could?
- Which color combo feels most "you"?

Use this space to draw your idea - have fun and sketch without overthinking!

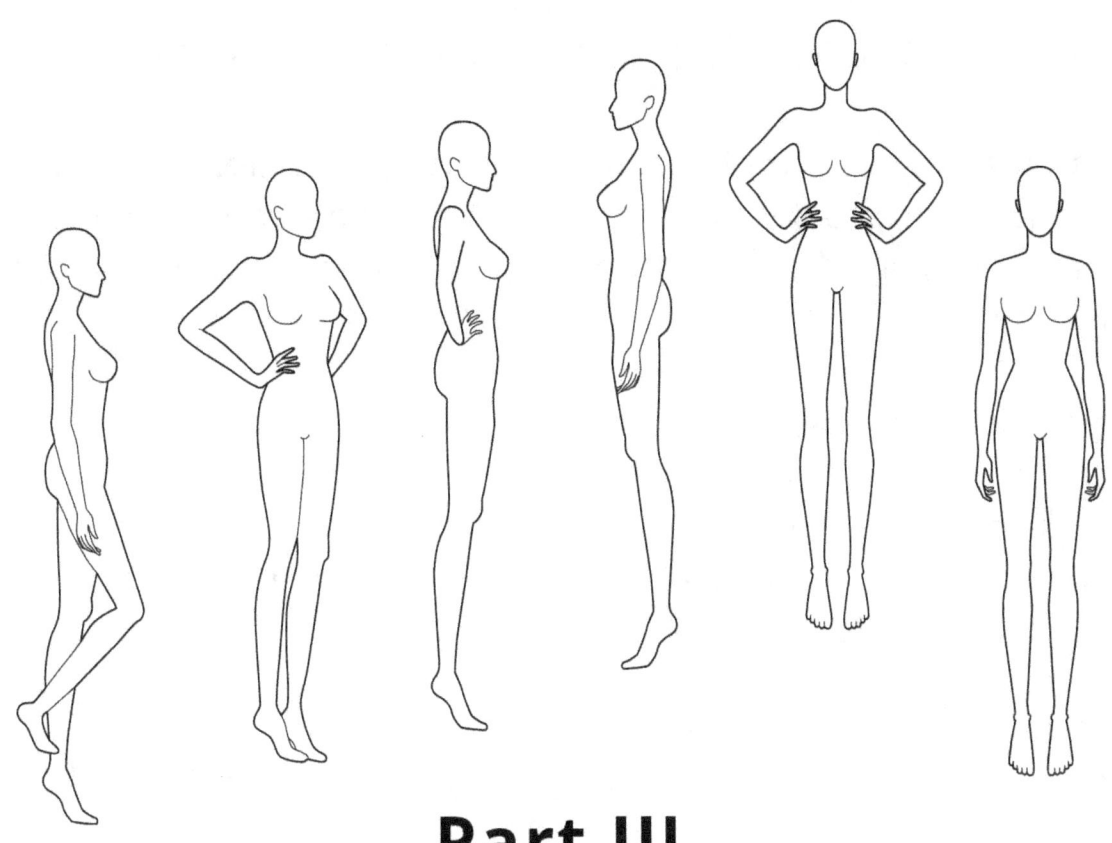

Part III
– Sketchbook & Practice

This is where your creativity truly takes off.

You've learned the basics - now it's time to explore, draw, and create your own fashion universe.

These pages are your playground: experiment, color, make mistakes, and most importantly - have fun.

Fashion Practice Guide & Notes

Fashion design is about exploration, not perfection. Use this page to try something bold - even if it feels outside your comfort zone. Mistakes are part of growth, and every sketch teaches you something new.

How to Use This Page:
- Experiment with proportions you don't usually draw.
- Add layers to see how fabrics interact.
- Use notes to describe movement or flow in the outfit.

Reflection & Notes:
- What new technique did I try today?
- Did the design feel balanced?
- Which detail could I refine in the next sketch?

Pro Tip: *Bold experiments often lead to your most original ideas.*

_____
_____
_____
_____
_____
_____
_____
_____
_____

Outfit Inspiration: Streetwear

The Power of Layering

Streetwear is all about layering-it's fun, creative, and gives you endless outfit combos. Start with a chill base like a tank top or crop tee, then build up with oversized hoodies, denim jackets, or flannel shirts. Try tying one layer around your waist or adding a hoodie under a trench coat. Each piece changes the whole vibe.

Play with opposites: soft fabrics under something structured, or mix bold prints with calm neutrals. Layering isn't just about style-it's practical too, perfect for changing weather or moods.

Try this: Sketch an outfit starting with a basic tee and cargo pants, then add a zip-up hoodie, oversized jacket, and sneakers. Notice how every new layer adds personality.

Trends

Inspiration

Textiles

Notes

Details

Swatches

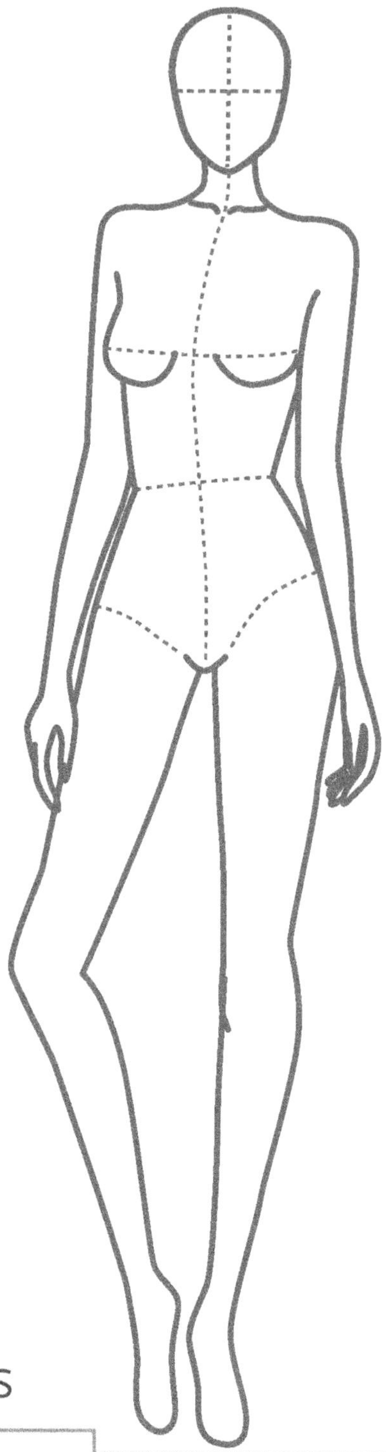

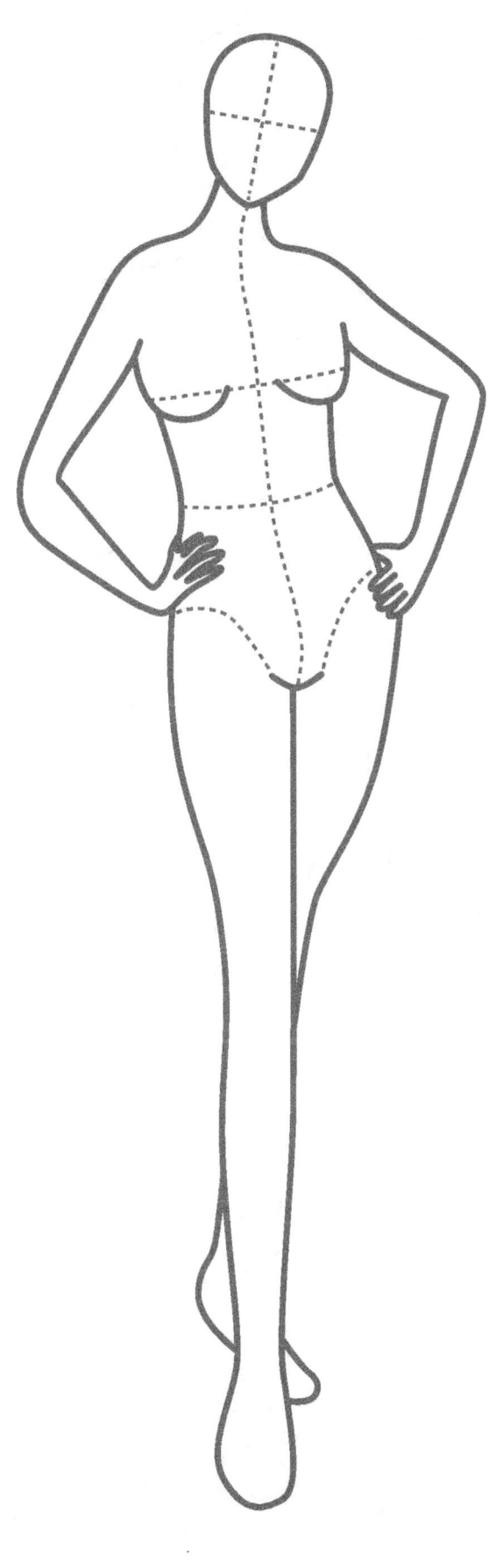
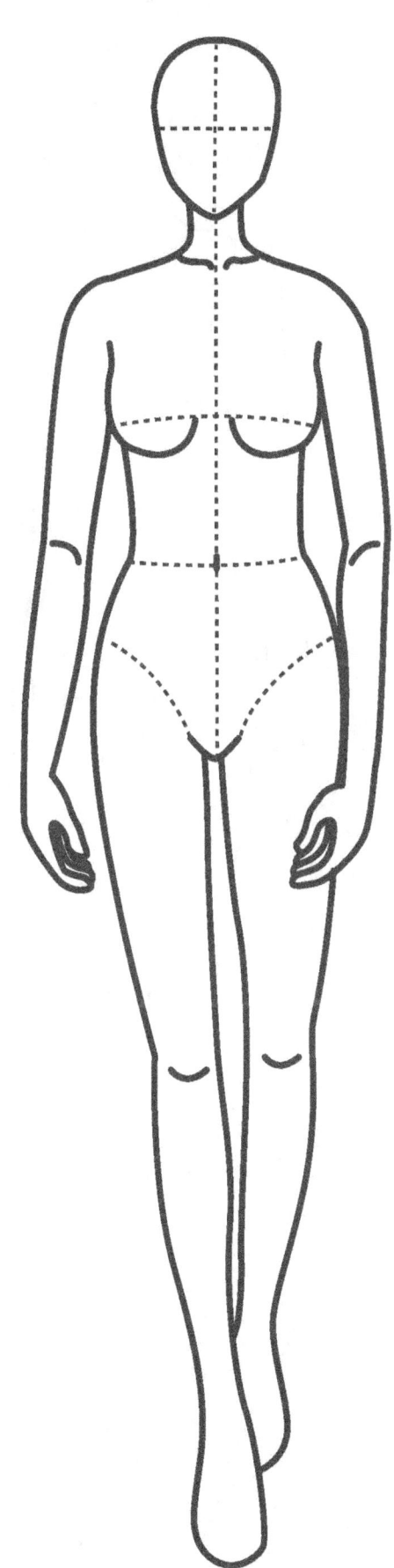

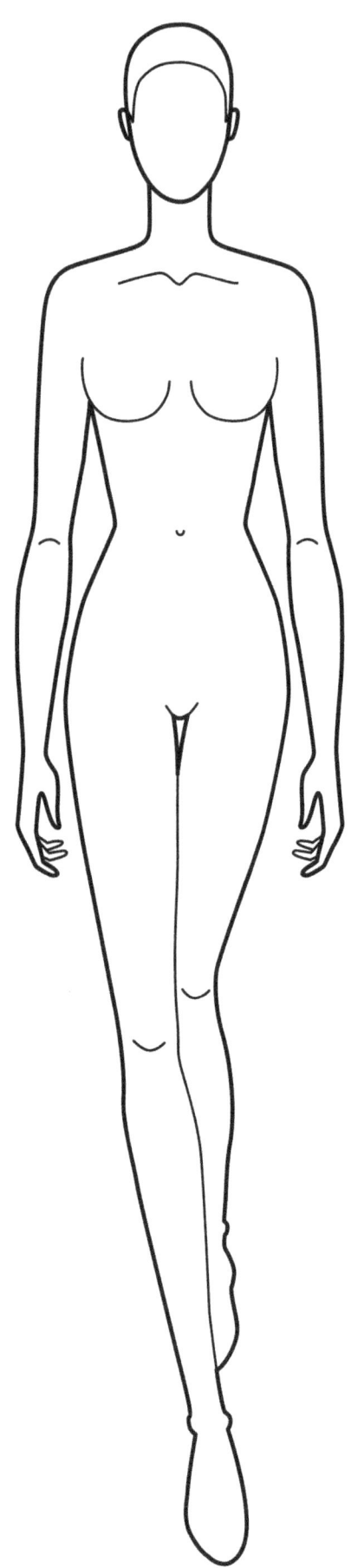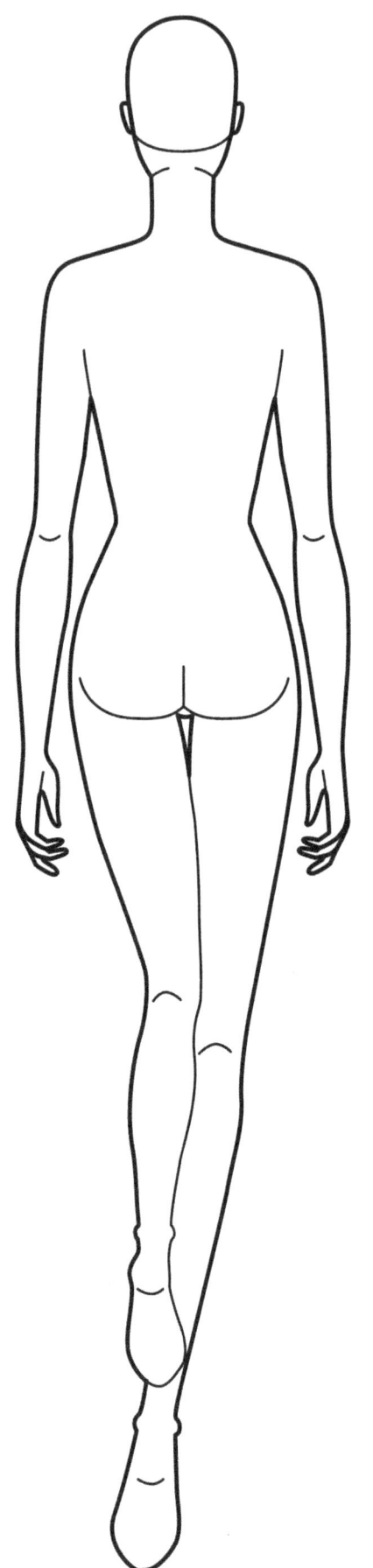

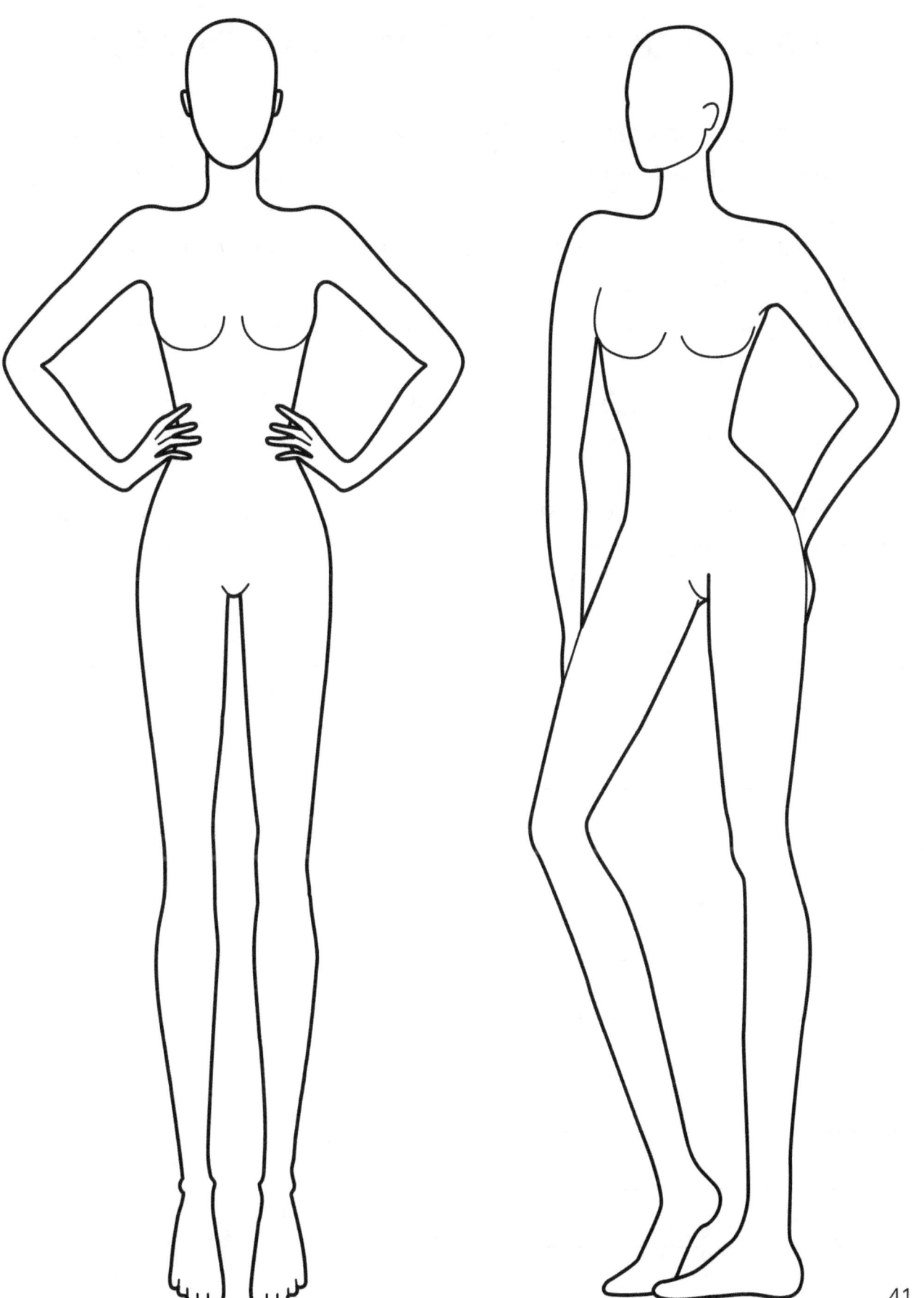

Your Notes & Inspiration Photos

This page is your creative gallery. Use it to track your progress, capture your favorite designs, and reflect on your journey.

- Add sketches, inspiration photos, or cutouts to bring your fashion ideas to life.
- Write down details such as colors, fabrics, or outfit elements that inspired you.
- Leave space for your future self to revisit and compare how your style evolves.

Pro Tip: *A single image or swatch can spark a whole collection. Don't be afraid to save even the smallest details that inspire you.*

Outfit Inspiration: School Chic & Party Glam

School Chic Inspiration

Think everyday outfits that still show your personality. Try a pleated skirt with a cropped sweater, or wide jeans with a tucked-in graphic tee and sneakers. Add a light jacket or blazer to make it look effortless but stylish. Accessories like layered necklaces or cool backpacks complete the look.

Party Glam Inspiration

For special occasions or weekend fun, go for sparkle and flow. Metallic skirts, sequined tops, or slip dresses with platform shoes feel playful and bold. Add statement jewelry or a mini bag for extra shine. The goal: look confident, have fun, and make every outfit feel like a moment.

Fashion Practice Guide & Notes

Design doesn't have to be perfect-it's about experimenting! Try to sketch quickly and see what comes out naturally.

How to Use This Page:
- Do a 5-minute warm-up sketch.
- Focus on one thing (like sleeves or shoes).
- Add notes about color, texture, or shape.

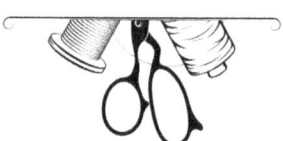

Reflection & Notes:
- Did drawing fast help me be more creative?
- What detail do I like best?
- What would I change next time?

Pro Tip: *Fast sketches help you loosen up and think like a real designer.*

_____
_____
_____
_____
_____
_____
_____
_____

Outfit Inspiration: Streetwear

Athleisure Energy: Sporty and Cool

Athleisure is comfort with attitude. Picture joggers with crop tops, oversized hoodies, or sporty zip jackets. Keep it relaxed but balanced-baggy pants with fitted tops, or the opposite.

Add fun accessories: bucket hats, chunky sneakers, crossbody mini bags.

Fabric focus: cotton blends, spandex, and lightweight knits. Add one shiny or colorful piece to make the outfit pop.

Pro Tip: Design an outfit that could go straight from class to the weekend-cool, comfy, and confident.

Trends

Inspiration

Textiles

Notes

Details

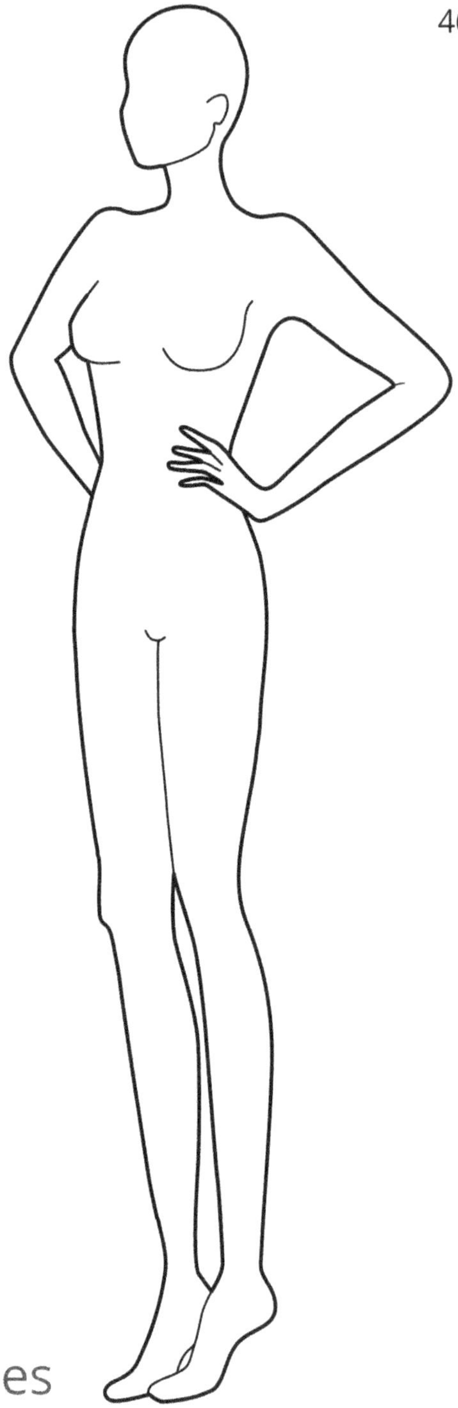

Swatches

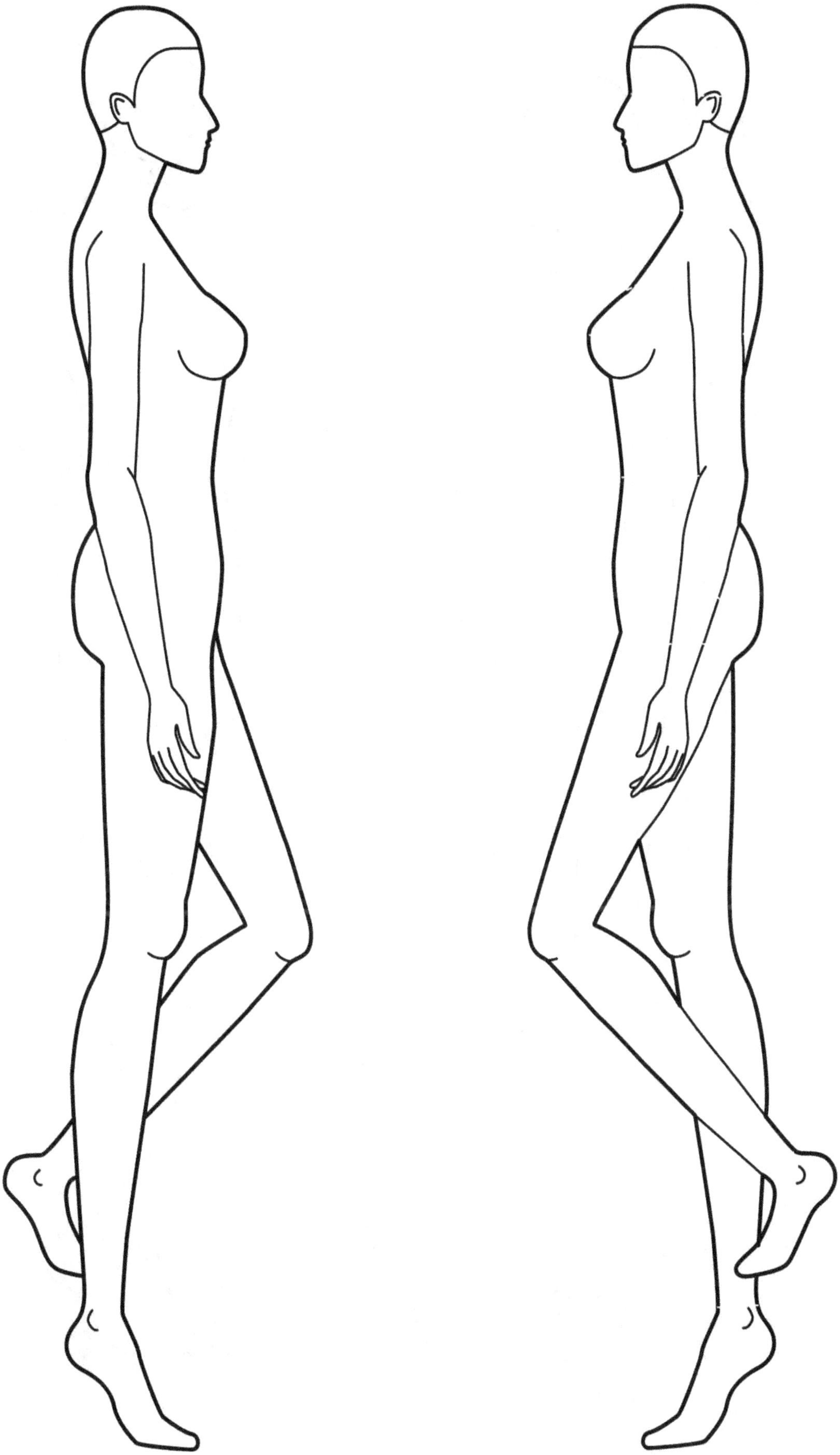

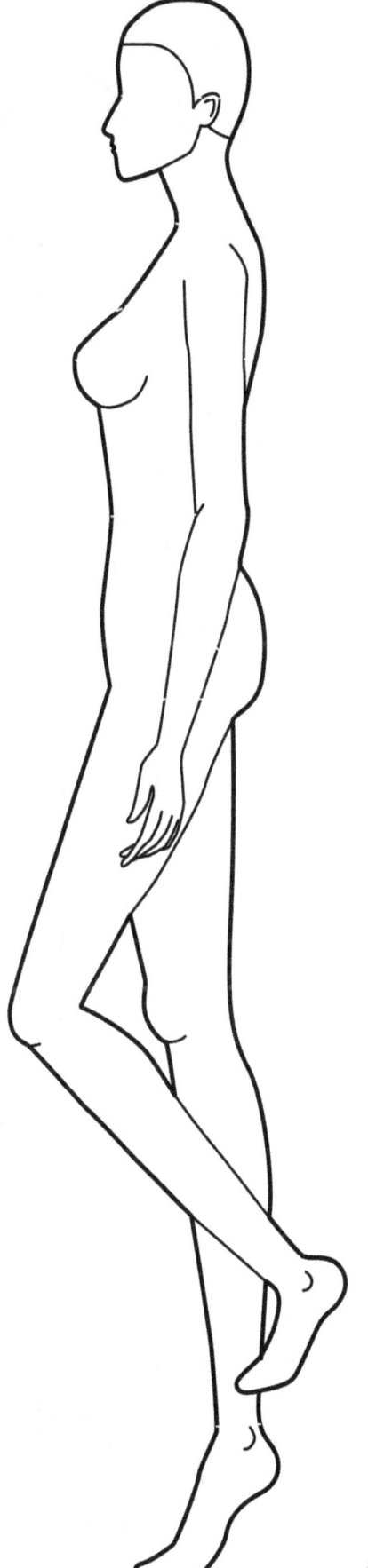

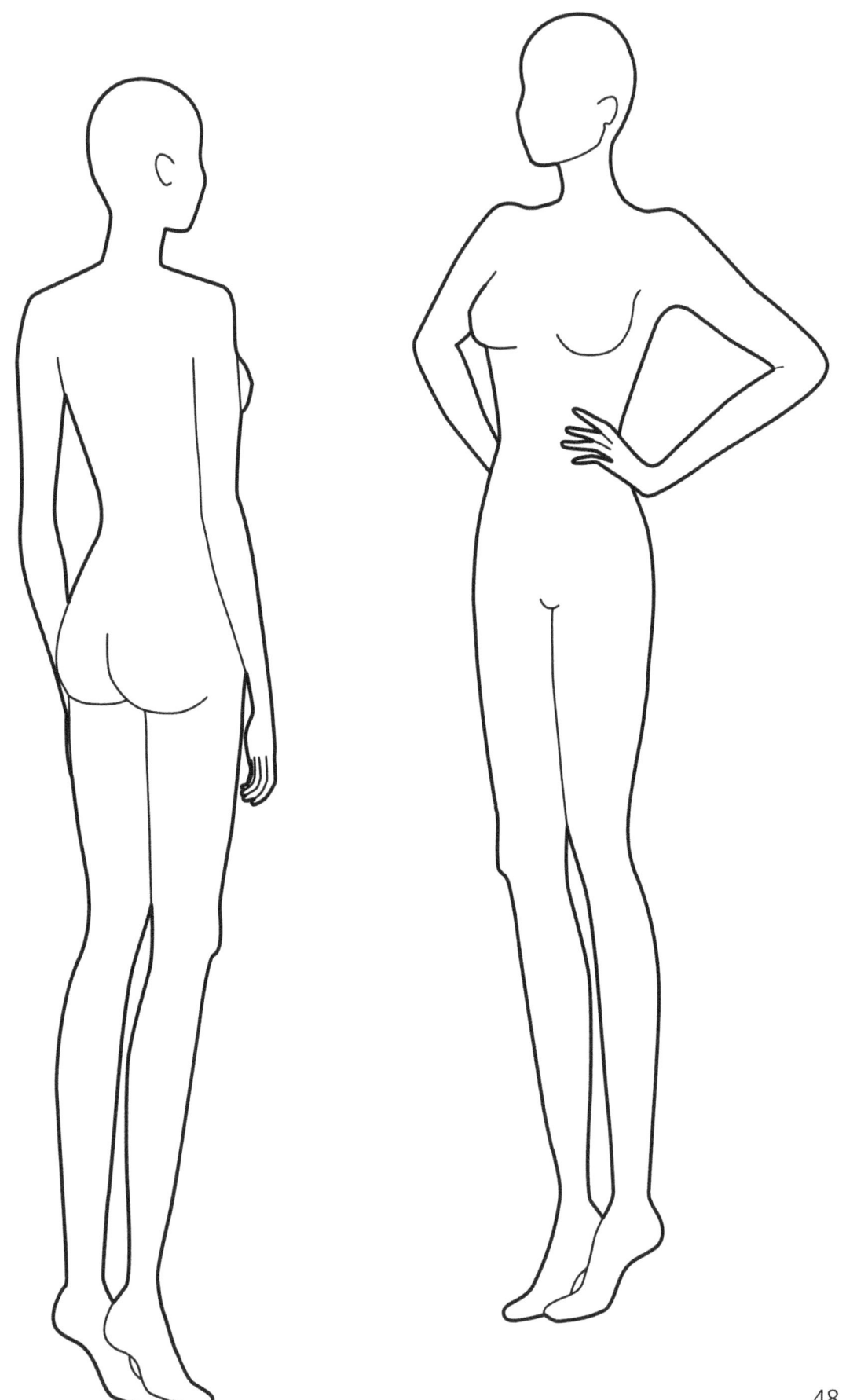

Your Notes & Inspiration Photos

This page is your creative gallery. Use it to track your progress, capture your favorite designs, and reflect on your journey.

- Add sketches, inspiration photos, or cutouts to bring your fashion ideas to life.
- Write down details such as colors, fabrics, or outfit elements that inspired you.
- Leave space for your future self to revisit and compare how your style evolves.

Pro Tip: *A single image or swatch can spark a whole collection. Don't be afraid to save even the smallest details that inspire you.*

Outfit Inspiration: School Smart & Futuristic Vibes

School Smart Inspiration

Think "cool but put-together." Wide-leg pants, simple tops, and light blazers or cardigans work perfectly. Add color pops-pastels or muted brights-to make it fun. Shoes can be sneakers, loafers, or ankle boots. It's smart, stylish, and easy to wear.

Futuristic Vibes Inspiration

Futuristic fashion is all about metallic touches and strong shapes. Imagine silver jackets, holographic fabrics, or geometric accessories. Keep the look bold but balanced-mix shiny textures with simple pieces. This style screams creativity and confidence.

Fashion Practice Guide & Notes

Fashion always tells a story. Use this page to design something inspired by your mood, favorite song, or even a movie.

How to Use This Page:
- Pick a theme (like confidence, travel, or friendship).
- Turn that idea into shapes, lines, and colors.
- Add details that make your outfit feel personal.

Reflection & Notes:
- Did my sketch match the feeling I wanted?
- Which detail tells my story best?
- What could make it even more "me"?

Pro Tip: *Your best designs come from what inspires you most.*

_____

_____

_____

_____

_____

_____

_____

_____

_____

Outfit Inspiration: Streetwear

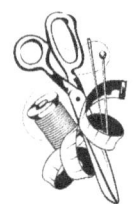

Denim Comeback: Classic Meets Cool

Denim never goes out of style. High-waisted jeans, cropped jackets, patchwork skirts-it all works! Mix light and dark washes, or double up on denim for a trendy twist.

Try this: Sketch an oversized denim jacket with wide jeans and a bright tee. Add sneakers, pins, or a cool belt to make it pop.

Customization is key: doodles, embroidery, or DIY patches can turn simple denim into your signature look.

Pro Tip: Denim is your canvas-make it as creative as you are.

Trends

Inspiration

Textiles

Notes

Details

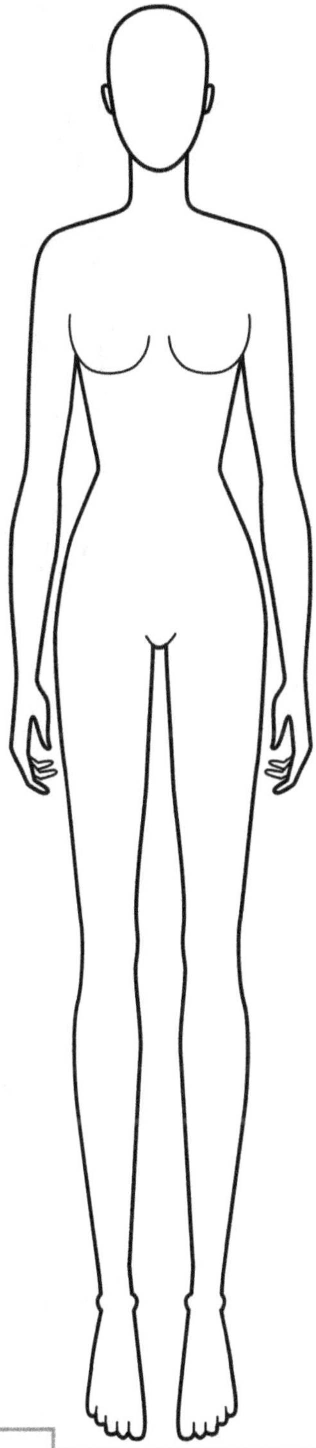

Swatches

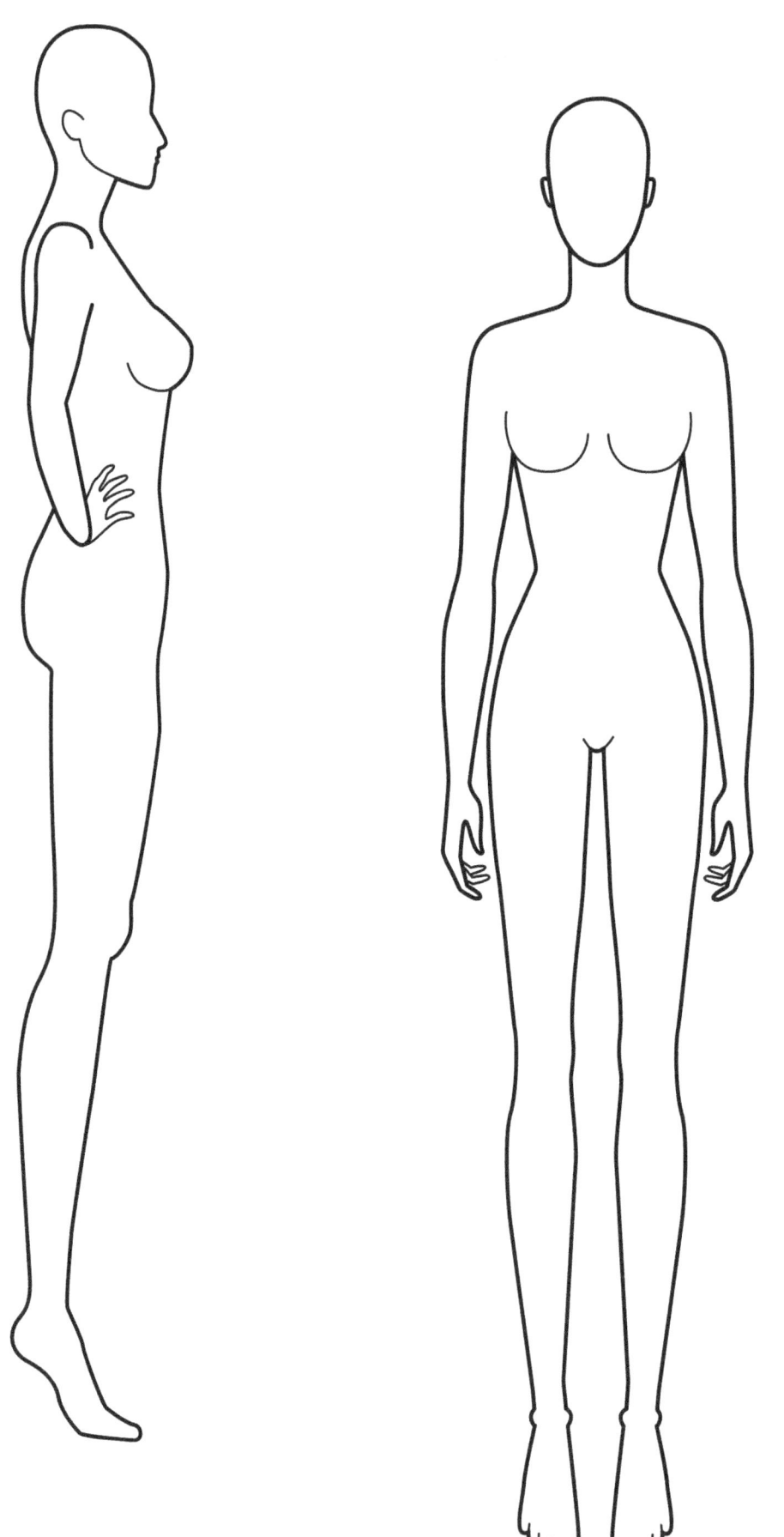

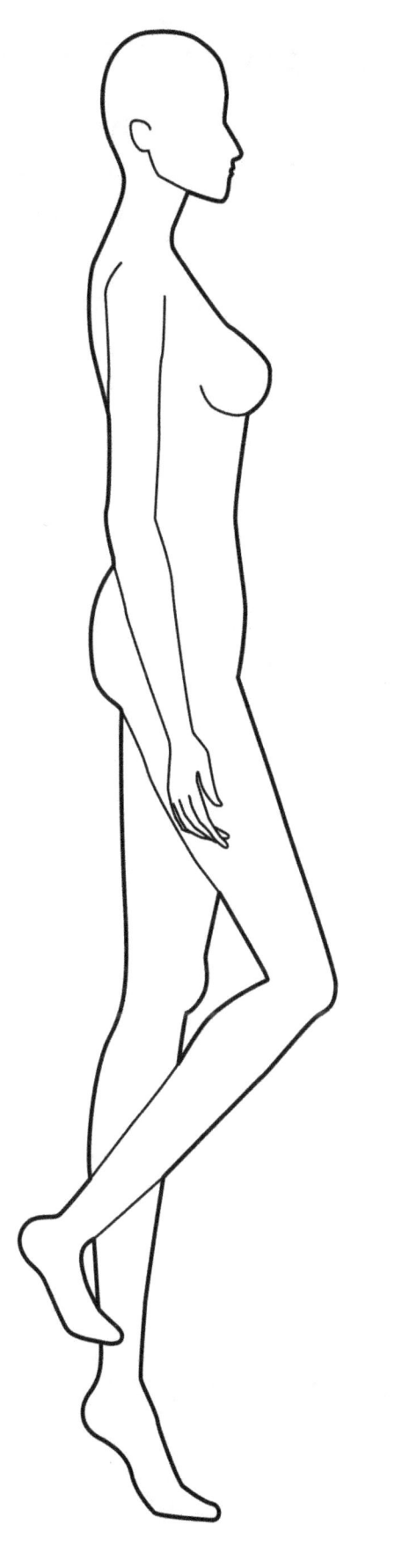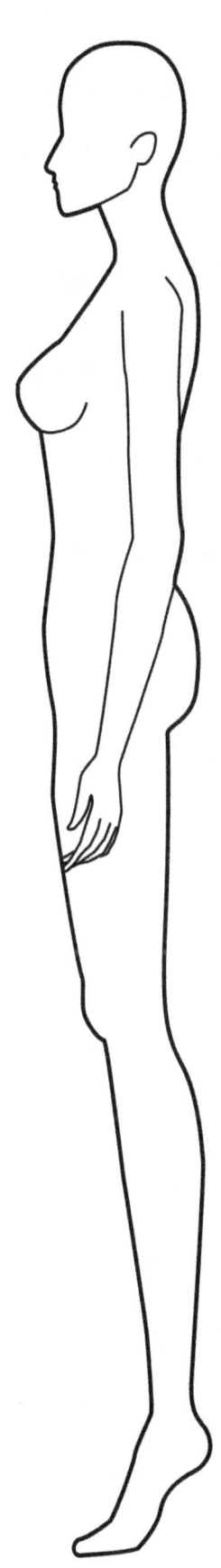

Your Notes & Inspiration Photos

This page is your creative gallery. Use it to track your progress, capture your favorite designs, and reflect on your journey.

- Add sketches, inspiration photos, or cutouts to bring your fashion ideas to life.
- Write down details such as colors, fabrics, or outfit elements that inspired you.
- Leave space for your future self to revisit and compare how your style evolves.

Pro Tip: *A single image or swatch can spark a whole collection. Don't be afraid to save even the smallest details that inspire you.*

Outfit Inspiration: Creative Campus & Festival Glam

Creative Campus Inspiration

Express yourself even on casual days. Go for patterned pants, graphic tees, or bold accessories. Oversized sweaters or long cardigans keep it cozy but stylish. Mix school-ready comfort with a creative edge.

Festival Glam Inspiration

Music, color, and freedom! Think flowy dresses, crop tops with fringe, and layered jewelry. Add metallic details or playful prints. This look is about joy and self-expression-perfect for sketching your dream summer outfit.

Fashion Practice Guide & Notes

Rules are made to be broken! Use this page to experiment with new combos or unexpected pairings.

How to Use This Page:
- Mix two styles (like sporty & elegant).
- Add accessories that change the outfit's mood.
- Write notes about what worked or didn't.

Reflection & Notes:
- Did I find a new style idea?
- What surprised me the most?
- Would I actually wear this outfit?

Pro Tip: *Great designers take risks. Try something bold today!*

_____
_____
_____
_____
_____
_____
_____
_____
_____

Outfit Inspiration: Streetwear

Oversized Energy: Play with Shape

Big silhouettes = big confidence. Picture an extra-large hoodie, cargo pants, or a slouchy denim jacket. Balance volume-loose tops with fitted bottoms, or crop tops with baggy pants.

Neutrals look classic, but one bright color or pastel makes it pop.

Pro Tip: *When you sketch, exaggerate the shapes a bit-it makes your design feel alive and bold.*

Trends

Inspiration

Textiles

Notes

Details

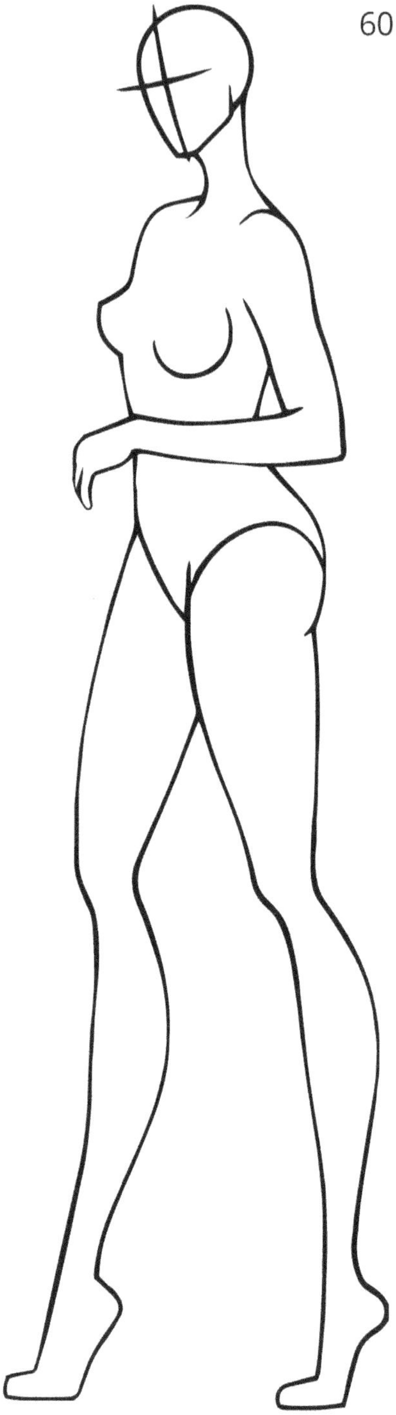

Swatches

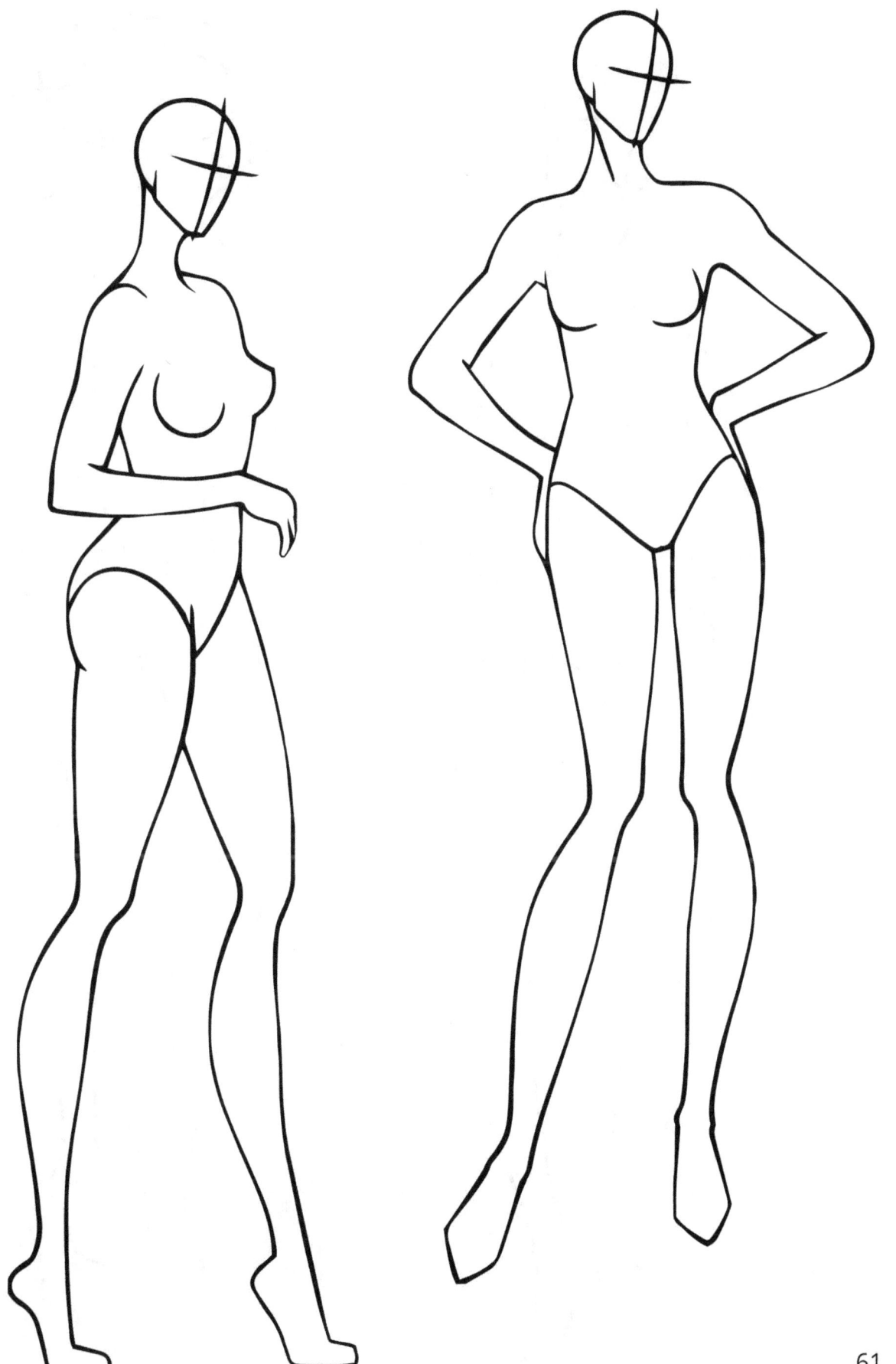

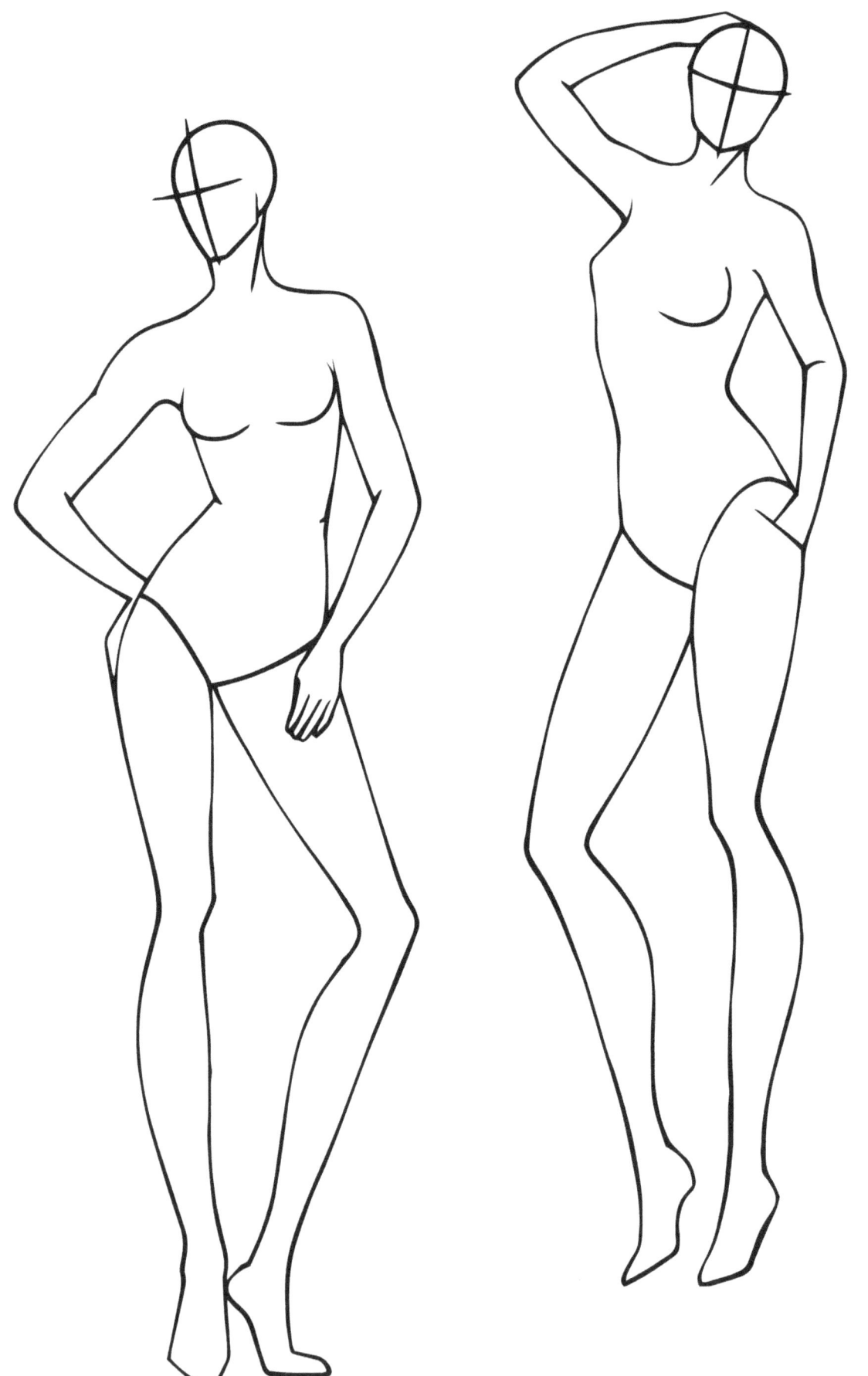

Your Notes & Inspiration Photos

This page is your creative gallery. Use it to track your progress, capture your favorite designs, and reflect on your journey.

- Add sketches, inspiration photos, or cutouts to bring your fashion ideas to life.
- Write down details such as colors, fabrics, or outfit elements that inspired you.
- Leave space for your future self to revisit and compare how your style evolves.

Pro Tip: *A single image or swatch can spark a whole collection. Don't be afraid to save even the smallest details that inspire you.*

Outfit Inspiration: Confident Daywear & Sustainable Glam

Confident Daywear Inspiration

Power dressing isn't just for adults-it's about feeling ready to take on the day. Try a fitted blazer over wide jeans, or a shirt dress with sneakers. Strong colors like emerald, plum, or navy show confidence without being too formal.

Sustainable Glam Inspiration

Fashion with purpose! Use eco-friendly ideas like recycled fabrics, thrifted details, or DIY customizations. Imagine a runway dress made from repurposed materials or hand-painted patterns. It's all about creativity that cares for the planet.

Fashion Practice Guide & Notes

Designs should look good and feel good. Think about how your outfit would work in real life.

How to Use This Page:
- Design for a situation (school, party, weekend trip).
- Imagine how the person moves in it.
- Add notes about comfort, fabrics, and fit.

Reflection & Notes:
- Is my outfit easy to wear?
- What makes it most practical?
- How can I make it more versatile?

Pro Tip: *The best designs mix comfort with creativity.*

_____
_____
_____
_____
_____
_____
_____
_____
_____

Outfit Inspiration: Streetwear

Graphic Attitude: Say It with Style

Your outfit can speak for you! Bold graphics and text show confidence and individuality. Try tees with slogans, hoodies with doodles, or jackets with painted backs.

Design challenge: Sketch a hoodie and create your own back print-maybe your initials, a phrase, or a symbol that represents you.

Fabric tip: In real life, you can use screen printing or patches-but on paper, your imagination is unlimited!

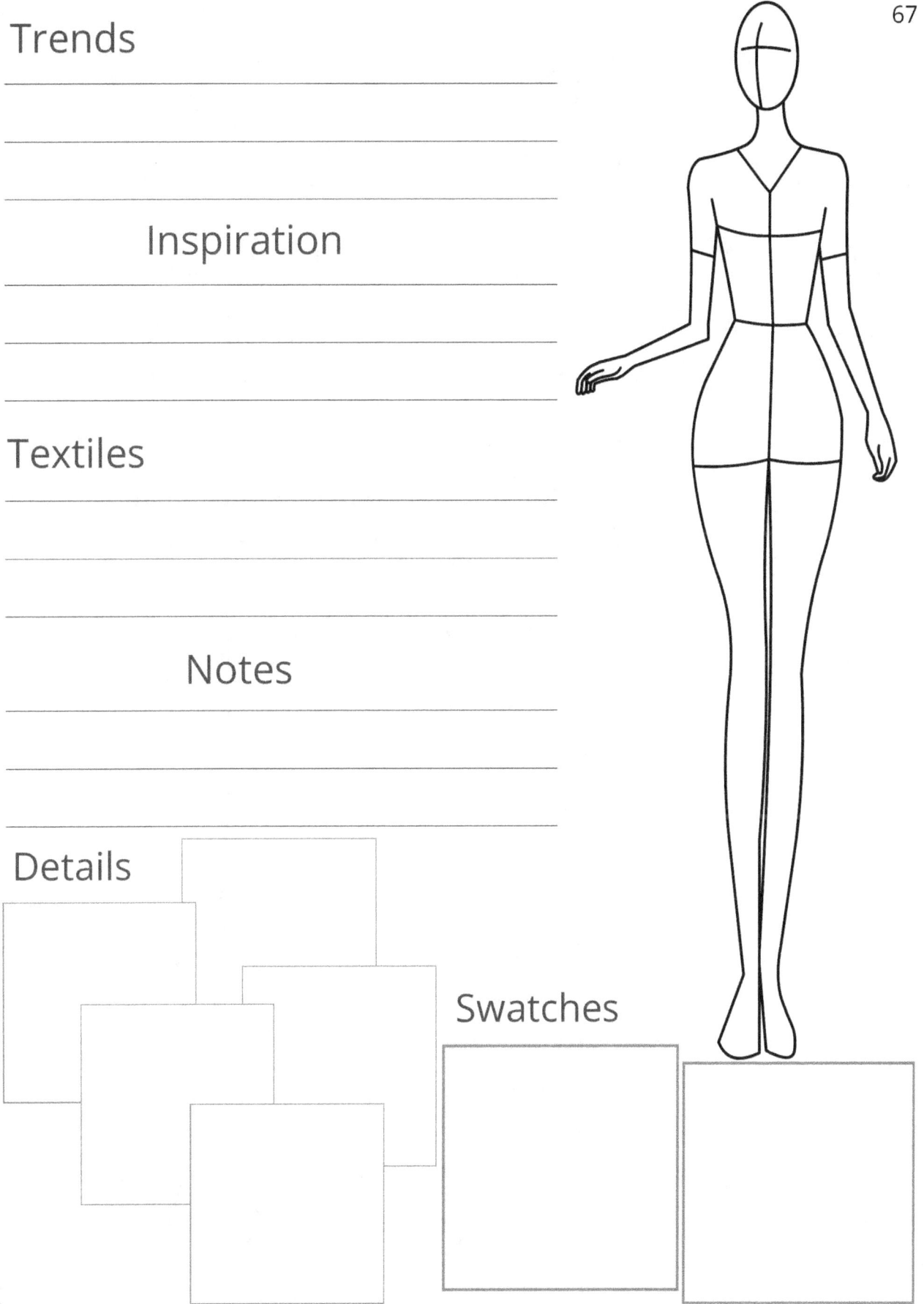

Trends

Inspiration

Textiles

Notes

Details

Swatches

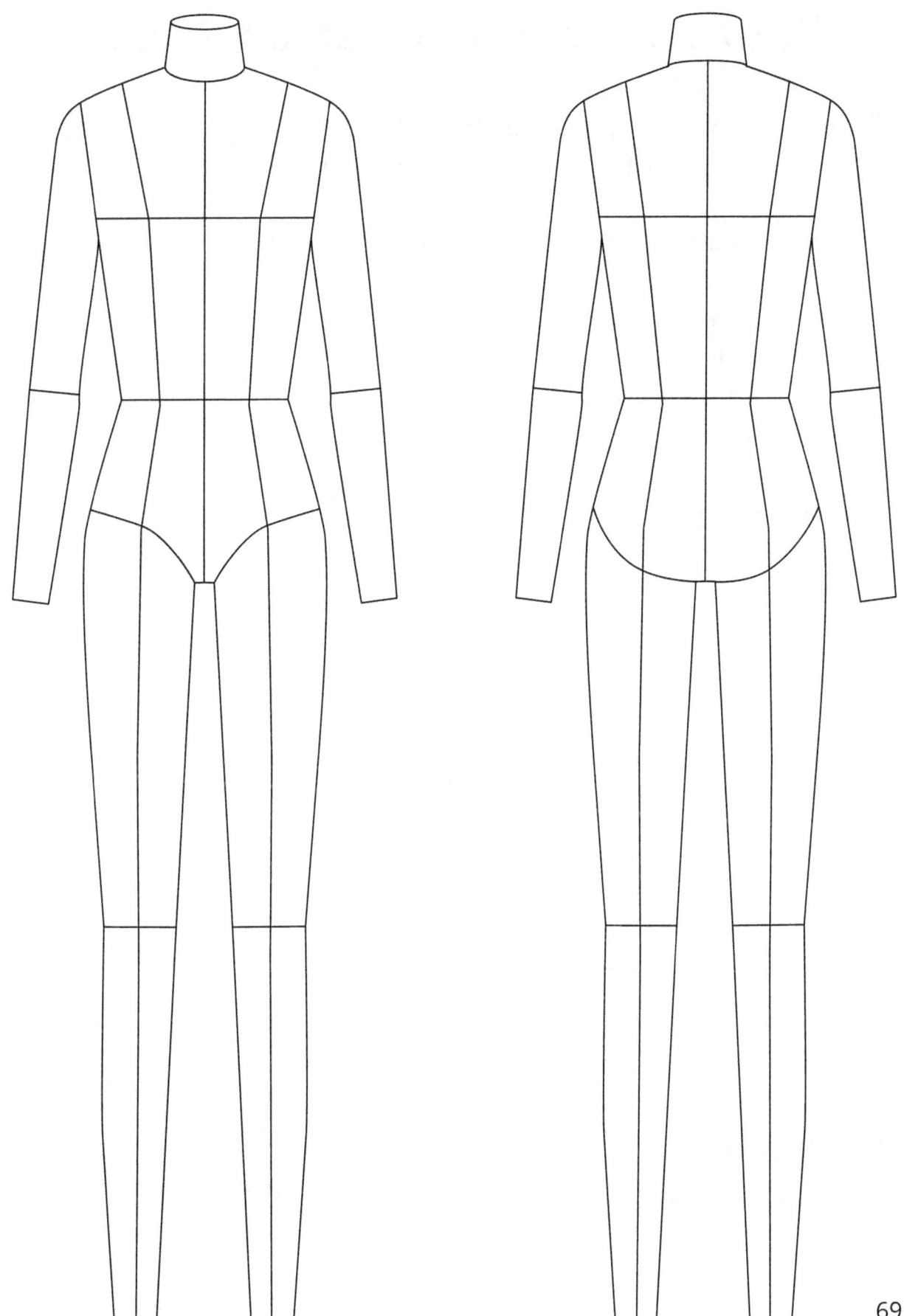

Your Notes & Inspiration Photos

This page is your creative gallery. Use it to track your progress, capture your favorite designs, and reflect on your journey.

- Add sketches, inspiration photos, or cutouts to bring your fashion ideas to life.
- Write down details such as colors, fabrics, or outfit elements that inspired you.
- Leave space for your future self to revisit and compare how your style evolves.

Pro Tip: *A single image or swatch can spark a whole collection. Don't be afraid to save even the smallest details that inspire you.*

Outfit Inspiration: Casual Friday & Couture Dream

Casual Friday Inspiration

Smart but chill-think jeans with a cute top and sneakers or ankle boots. Add a blazer for structure or swap it for a denim jacket for a relaxed twist. Keep accessories simple but stylish.

Couture Dream Inspiration

Think big, dramatic, and full of personality! Imagine a flowing gown, metallic fabrics, or oversized bows. Haute couture isn't about rules-it's about imagination. Design something that feels luxurious and original.

Fashion Practice Guide & Notes

Textures make your designs stand out!

How to Use This Page:
- Sketch an outfit and label your fabric ideas.
- Mix soft and structured textures.
- Write how each fabric should move or feel.

Reflection & Notes:
- Which texture combo works best?
- Did I balance softness and structure?
- How can I make it look more realistic?

Pro Tip: *The right texture turns a flat sketch into fashion magic.*

_____
_____
_____
_____
_____
_____
_____
_____
_____
_____

Outfit Inspiration: Streetwear

Chill Neutrals

Neutral doesn't mean boring! Beige, grey, white, and black can look super fresh when styled right. Try joggers with a crop top, or an oversized coat with sneakers. Add one accent color-like red or neon green-to bring the outfit to life.

Sketch idea: Design an all-neutral outfit, then add one bold detail and see how it changes the look.

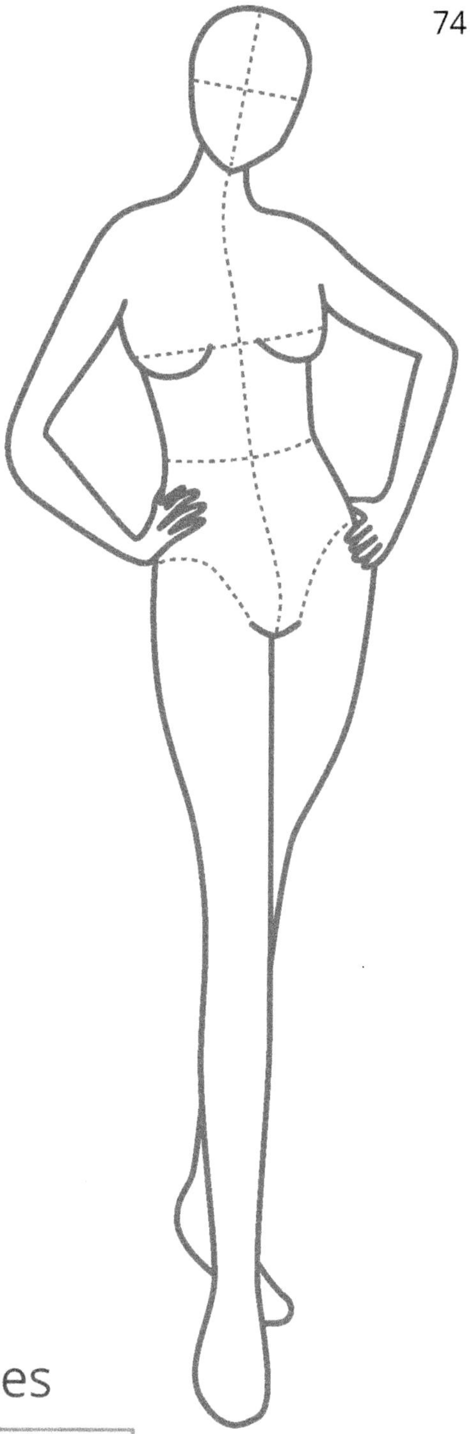

Trends

Inspiration

Textiles

Notes

Details

Swatches

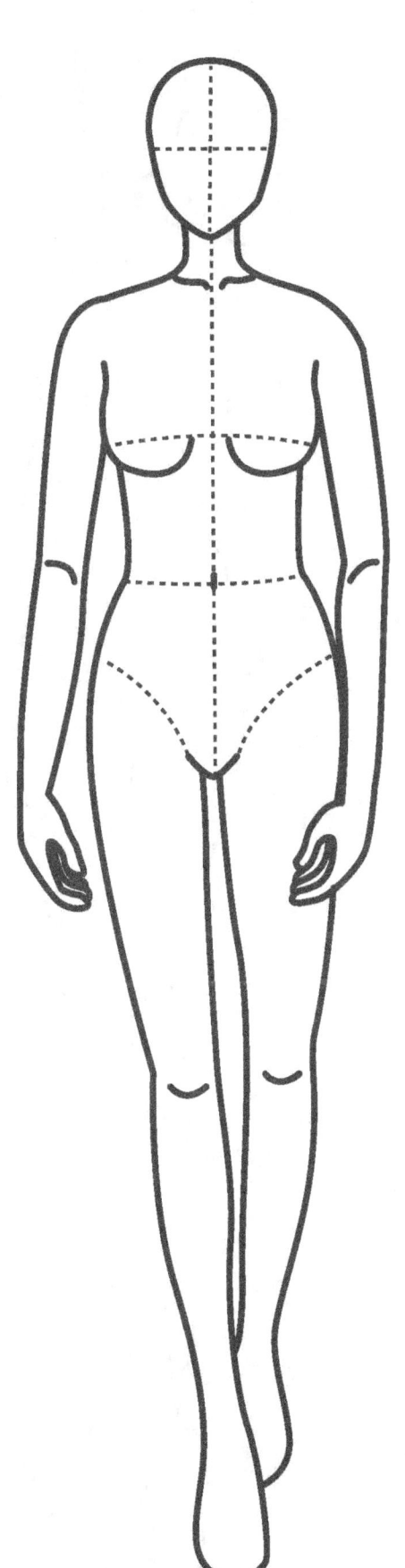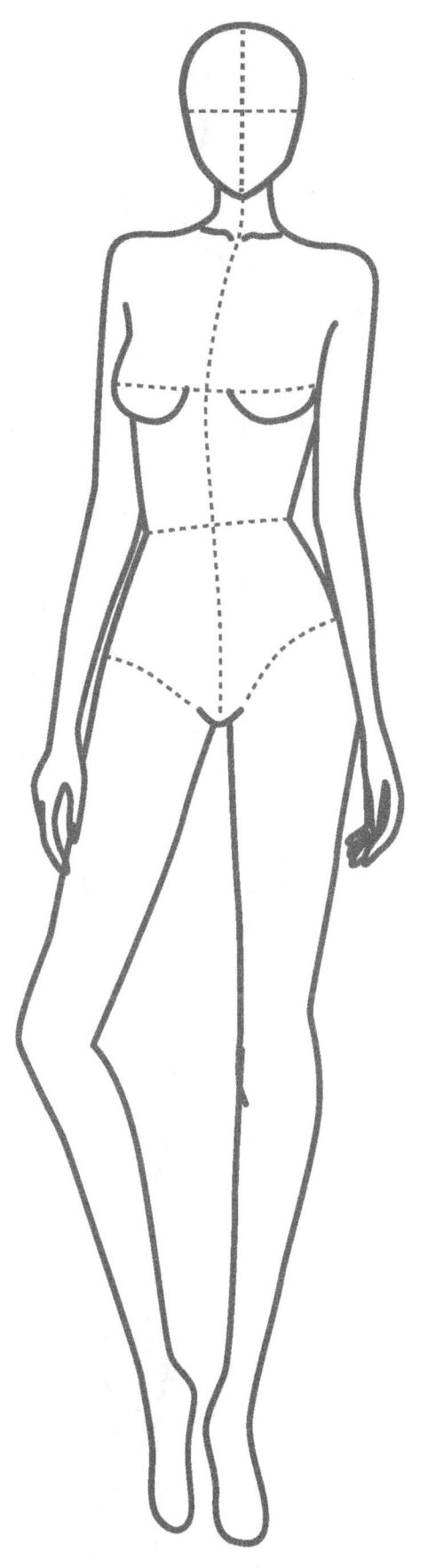

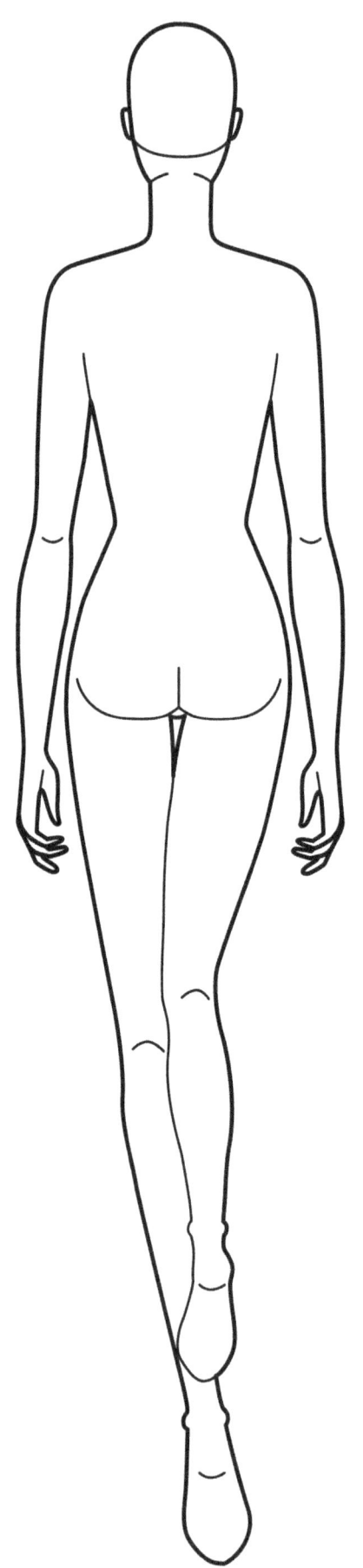
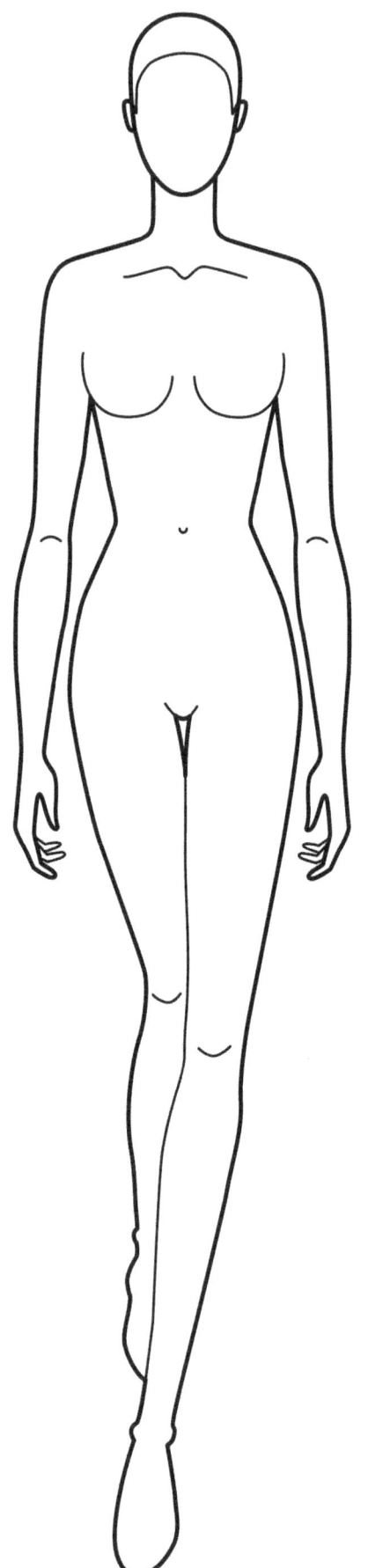

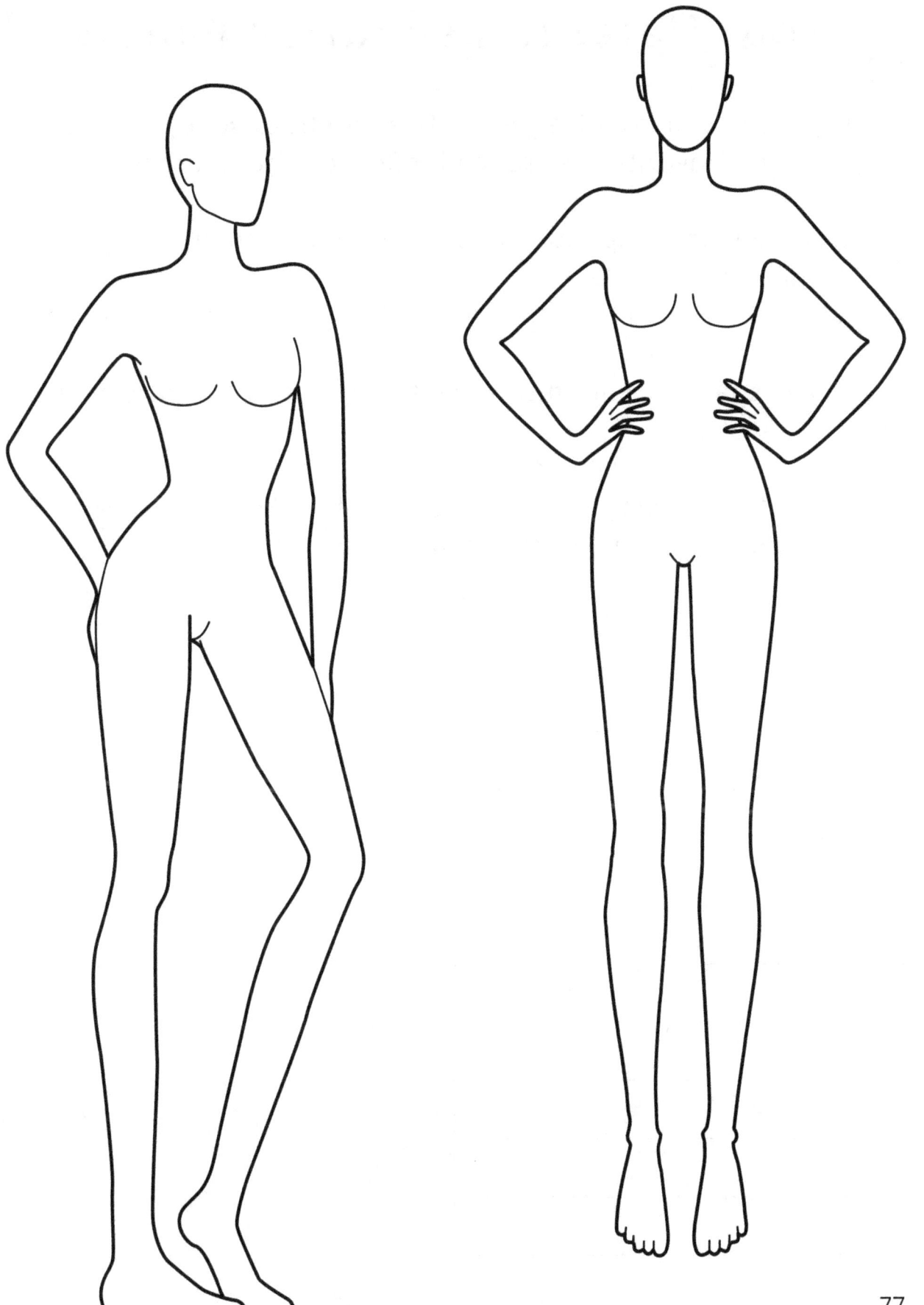

Your Notes & Inspiration Photos

This page is your creative gallery. Use it to track your progress, capture your favorite designs, and reflect on your journey.

- Add sketches, inspiration photos, or cutouts to bring your fashion ideas to life.
- Write down details such as colors, fabrics, or outfit elements that inspired you.
- Leave space for your future self to revisit and compare how your style evolves.

Pro Tip: *A single image or swatch can spark a whole collection. Don't be afraid to save even the smallest details that inspire you.*

Outfit Inspiration: Monochrome Mood & Minimal Glam

Monochrome Mood Inspiration

Pick one color and explore its shades-like sky blue to navy or blush to rose. Use different textures (knit, satin, denim) to keep it interesting. Monochrome looks calm but confident.

Minimal Glam Inspiration

Simple doesn't mean plain! Try clean lines, solid colors, and one standout accessory. Think a sleek jumpsuit with shiny earrings or a plain dress with a bright clutch.

Pro Tip:

Minimalism is timeless-let the silhouette shine.

Fashion Practice Guide & Notes

Accessories can totally change an outfit!

How to Use This Page:
- Start with a simple base outfit.
- Try adding 2–3 different accessory sets.
- Compare how each combo changes the mood.

Reflection & Notes:
- Which version feels most "me"?
- Did the accessories add or distract?
- How can I find balance next time?

Pro Tip: *Even the smallest accessory can make the biggest difference.*

_____

_____

_____

_____

_____

_____

_____

_____

_____

Outfit Inspiration: Streetwear

Streetwear with a Feminine Twist

Streetwear doesn't always have to look sporty or tomboyish. You can make it softer and more playful by mixing in girly details-like pairing a mini skirt with sneakers or layering a slip dress over a tee.

Try fabrics and textures: mix satin skirts with hoodies, or denim shorts with lace tops. Blending casual and delicate gives your outfit balance and personality.

Sketch Challenge: Create a look that combines something feminine (like a skirt or cute top) with a streetwear staple (like sneakers, joggers, or a hoodie).

Pro Tip: Real confidence comes from mixing what you love-don't worry about labels like "girly" or "tomboy." Just make it you.

Trends

Inspiration

Textiles

Notes

Details

Swatches

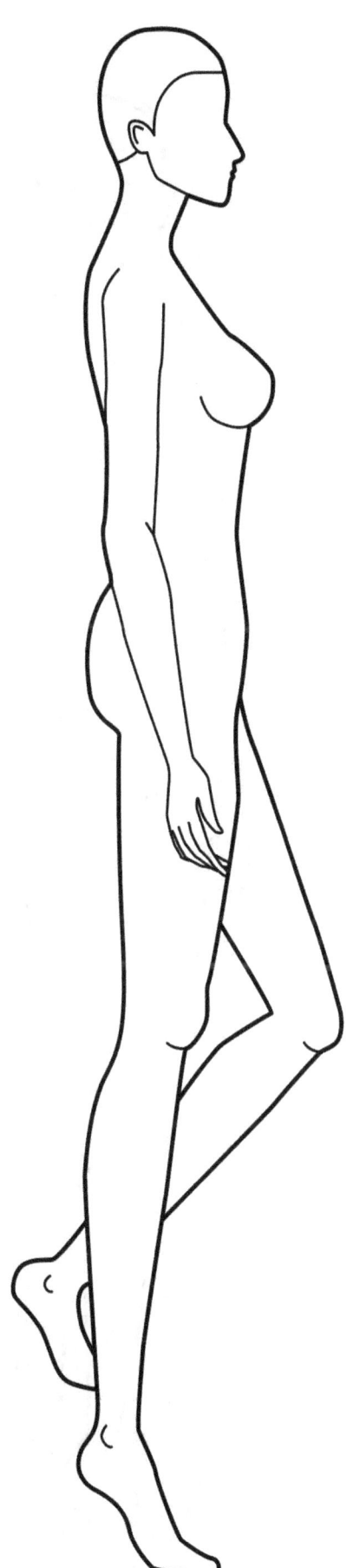
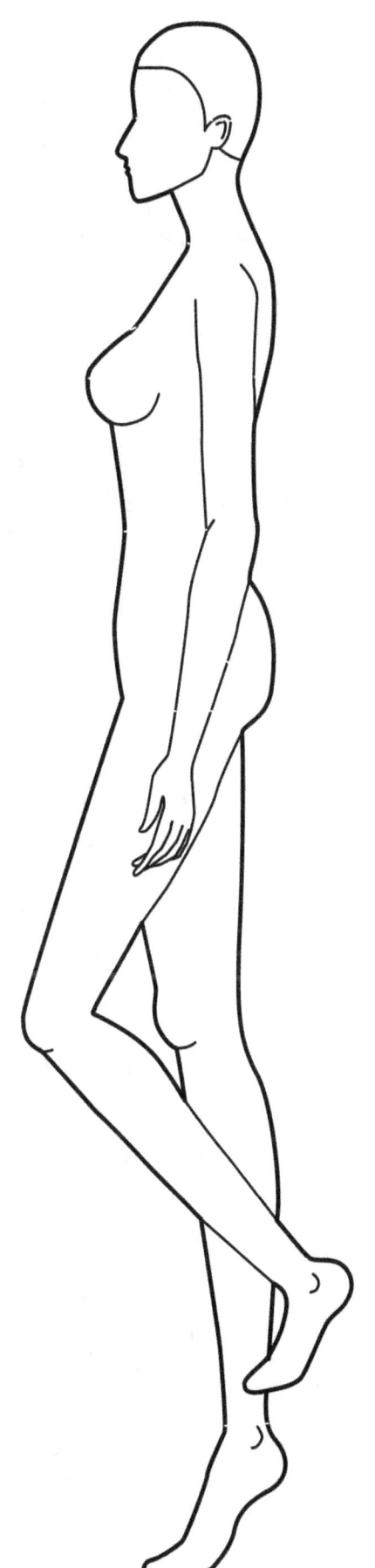

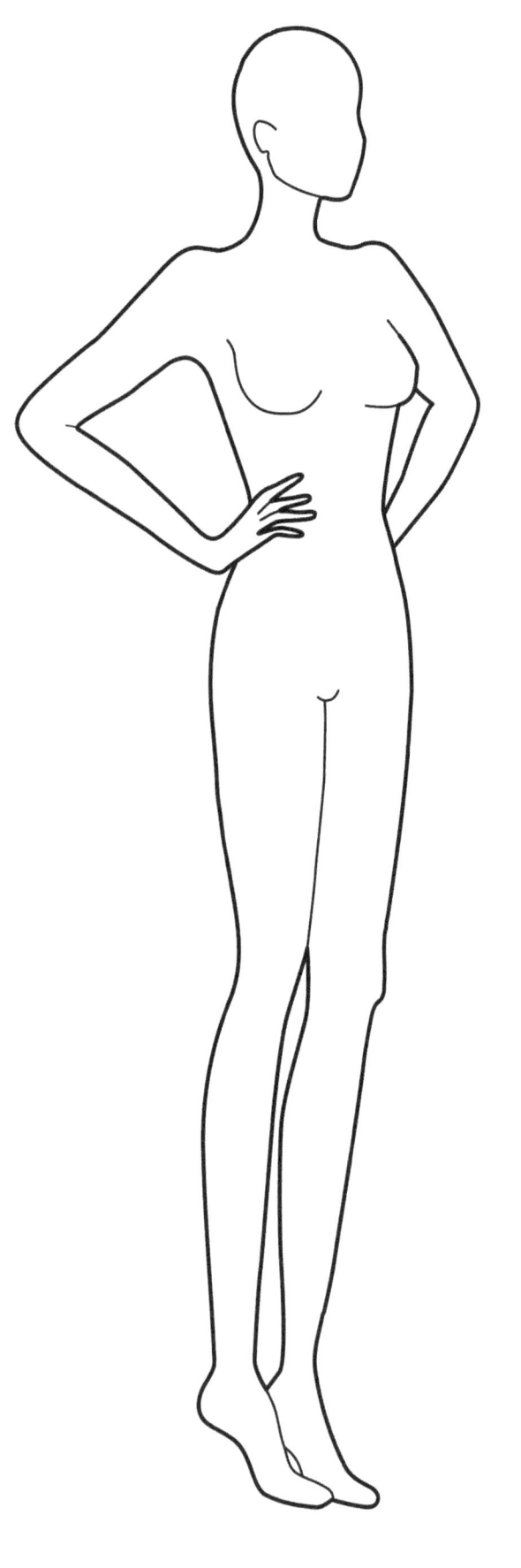
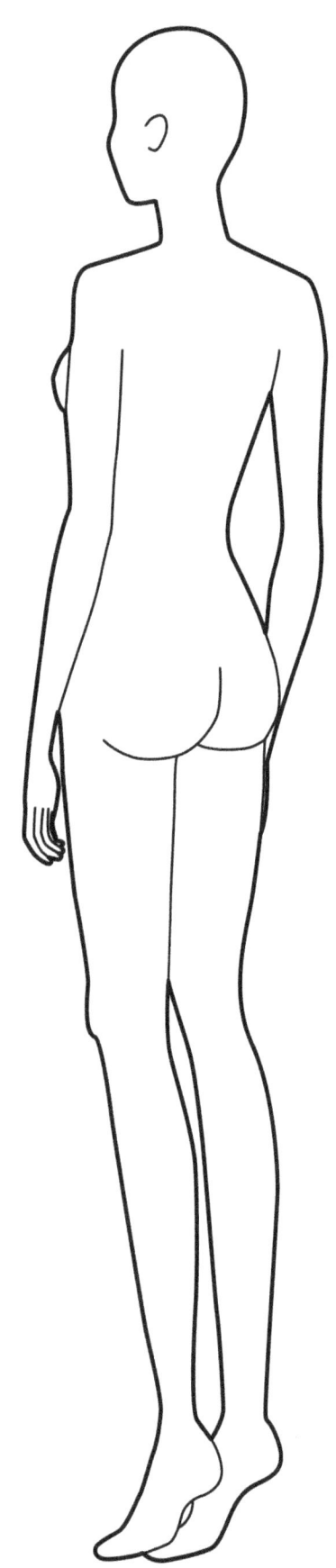

Your Notes & Inspiration Photos

This page is your creative gallery. Use it to track your progress, capture your favorite designs, and reflect on your journey.

- Add sketches, inspiration photos, or cutouts to bring your fashion ideas to life.
- Write down details such as colors, fabrics, or outfit elements that inspired you.
- Leave space for your future self to revisit and compare how your style evolves.

Pro Tip: *A single image or swatch can spark a whole collection. Don't be afraid to save even the smallest details that inspire you.*

Outfit Inspiration: School Smart & Futuristic Glam

School Smart Inspiration

Upgrade your "school look" with a touch of elegance. Try a blouse with soft ruffles, pleated skirts, or wide-leg pants in pastel colors. Pair them with neutral sneakers or loafers and simple accessories. It's classy but still totally wearable for your everyday routine.

Futuristic Glam Inspiration

Futuristic glam is where creativity meets shine. Picture soft flowing fabrics mixed with metallics or holographic details. Dresses with structured tops and airy skirts give that perfect contrast. Add chrome belts or geometric earrings for an out-of-this-world finish.

Pro Tip: *Think "sci-fi meets sparkle." Fashion can look futuristic and feminine at the same time!*

Fashion Practice Guide & Notes

Every design you sketch helps you improve proportions and flow.
This page is your training zone!

How to Use This Page:
- Focus on body balance-how long the torso and legs look.
- Notice how clothes fall naturally on the figure.
- Add notes on fit: relaxed, fitted, or oversized.

Reflection & Notes:
- Are my proportions better than before?
- Which part of my drawing feels most natural?
- How can I make my poses more realistic?

Pro Tip: *Good proportions make your fashion sketches look professional and dynamic.*

_____
_____
_____
_____
_____
_____
_____
_____

Outfit Inspiration: Streetwear

The Utility Trend: Function Meets Style

Utility fashion is practical and stylish. Think cargo pants, tactical vests, and belts with clips or big pockets-pieces inspired by workwear.

Color ideas: olive green, khaki, black, and camouflage tones.

Accessories like chunky boots, crossbody bags, or bucket hats complete the look.

Sketch Challenge: Design a cropped tank with baggy cargo pants and a utility vest. Add your favorite sneakers or combat boots for a powerful vibe.

Pro Tip: *Streetwear with purpose looks confident and strong.*

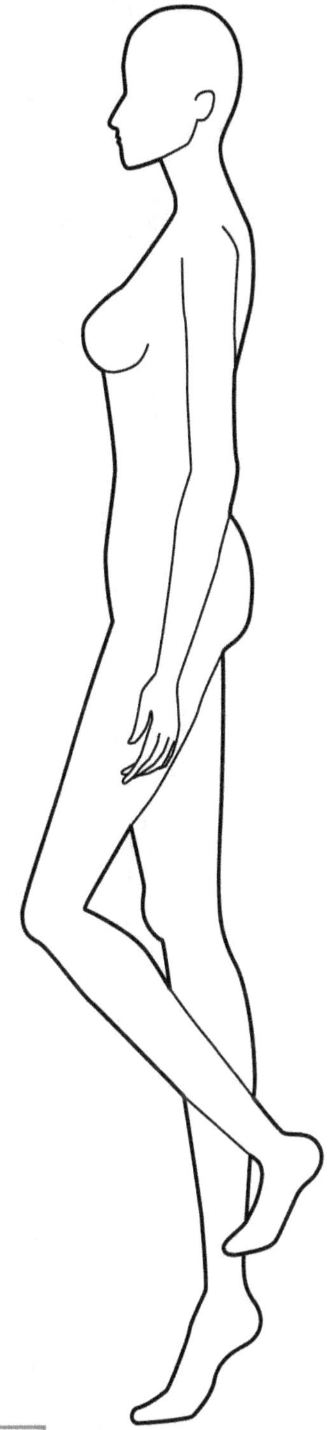

Trends

Inspiration

Textiles

Notes

Details

Swatches

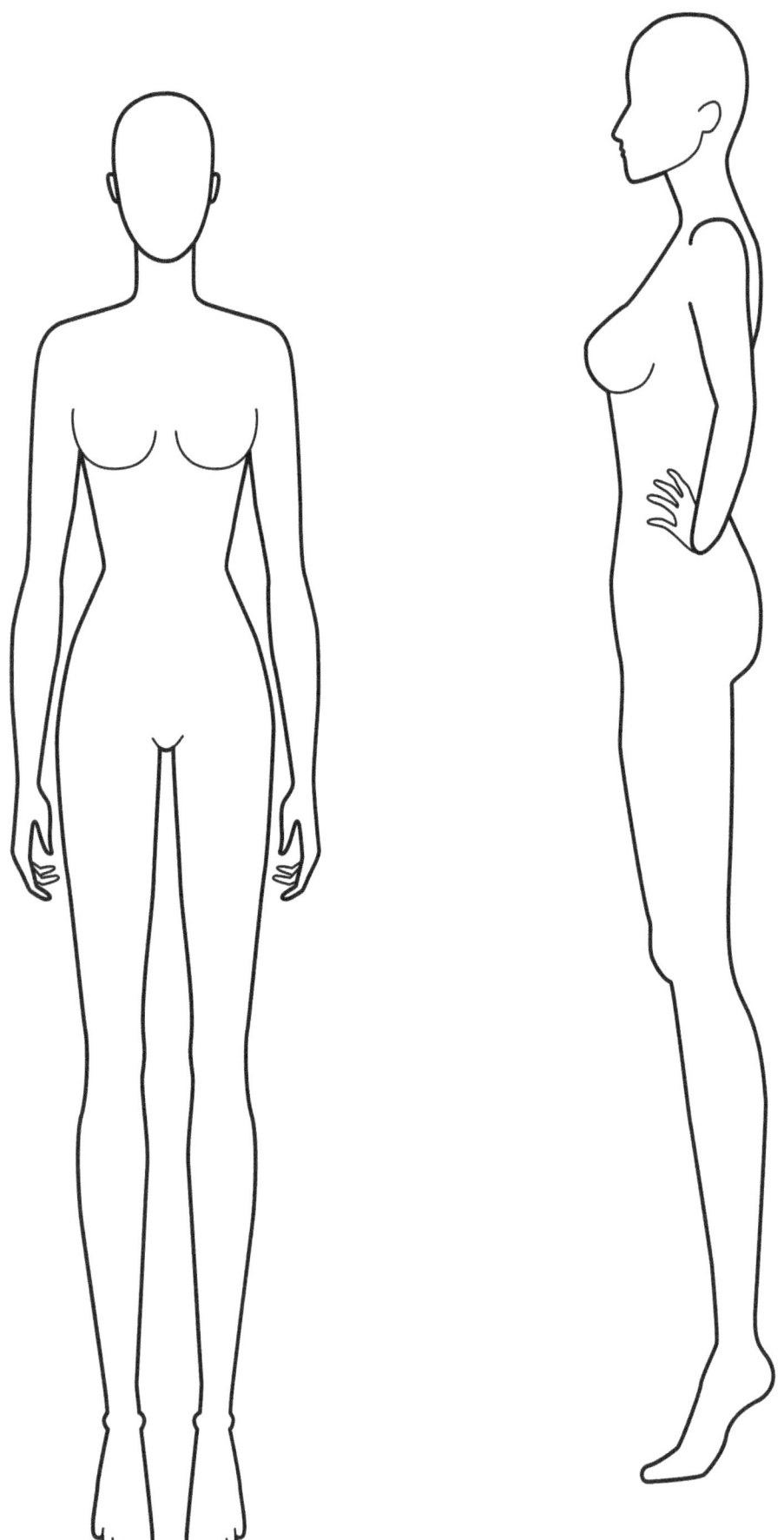

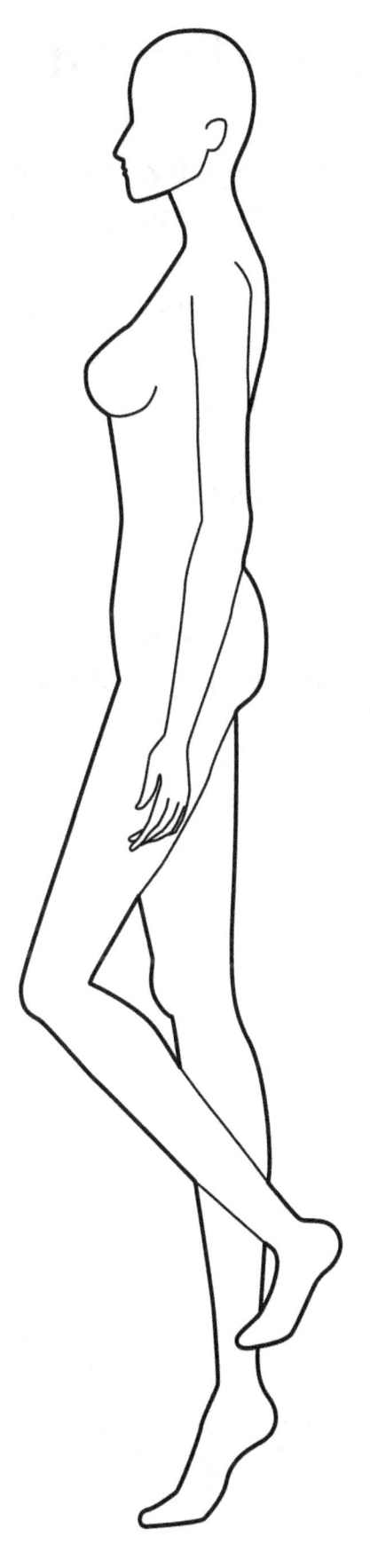
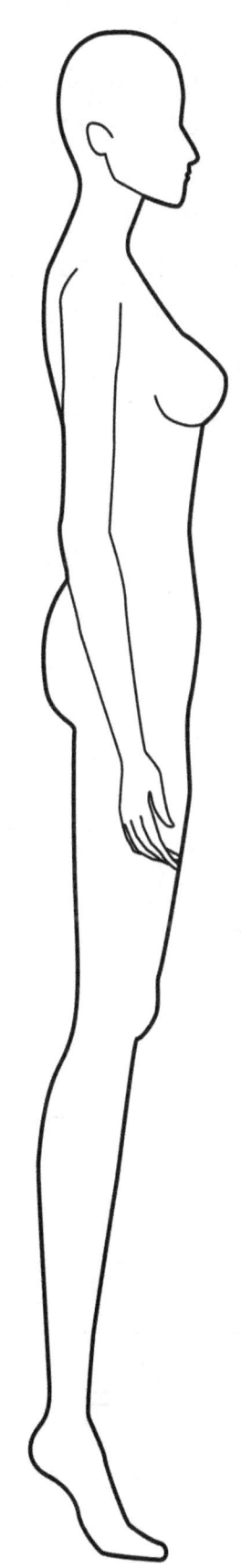

91

Your Notes & Inspiration Photos

This page is your creative gallery. Use it to track your progress, capture your favorite designs, and reflect on your journey.

- Add sketches, inspiration photos, or cutouts to bring your fashion ideas to life.
- Write down details such as colors, fabrics, or outfit elements that inspired you.
- Leave space for your future self to revisit and compare how your style evolves.

Pro Tip: *A single image or swatch can spark a whole collection. Don't be afraid to save even the smallest details that inspire you.*

Outfit Inspiration: Smart-Casual & Festival Sparkle

Smart-Casual Inspiration

Balance comfort and polish! Pair straight-cut pants with a tucked-in tee or sweater. Add a cropped blazer or lightweight jacket. Finish the look with sneakers or ankle boots-perfect for presentations or chill study sessions.

Festival Sparkle Inspiration

Festival glam is all about freedom and fun. Sequins, shimmer, and holographic fabrics bring color and excitement. Try flowy skirts, fringe details, or embellished tops. Add statement sunglasses or layered jewelry for extra shine.

Pro Tip: *Design an outfit that shines under sunlight or stage lights-let your creativity glow!*

Fashion Practice Guide & Notes

Colors tell a story-each one changes the whole outfit vibe.

How to Use This Page:
- Sketch one outfit and test 2–3 color palettes.
- Label them (warm, cool, or monochrome).
- See how the feeling changes with each.

Reflection & Notes:
- Which palette feels the most "me"?
- Do the colors clash or complement?
- How would I use these tones again?

Pro Tip: *Color is emotion-use it to express your mood and personality.*

_____
_____
_____
_____
_____
_____
_____
_____
_____

Outfit Inspiration: Streetwear

Vintage Streetwear Revival

Old-school is always cool! Streetwear often brings back trends from the 80s, 90s, and early 2000s-oversized denim, plaid shirts, tie-dye, or bucket hats.

Design idea: Remix a retro look with a modern twist. Maybe wide-leg jeans and a cropped hoodie, or a tie-dye sweatshirt with new-gen sneakers.

Pro Tip: *Fashion always comes back around-add your own touch to make vintage feel fresh.*

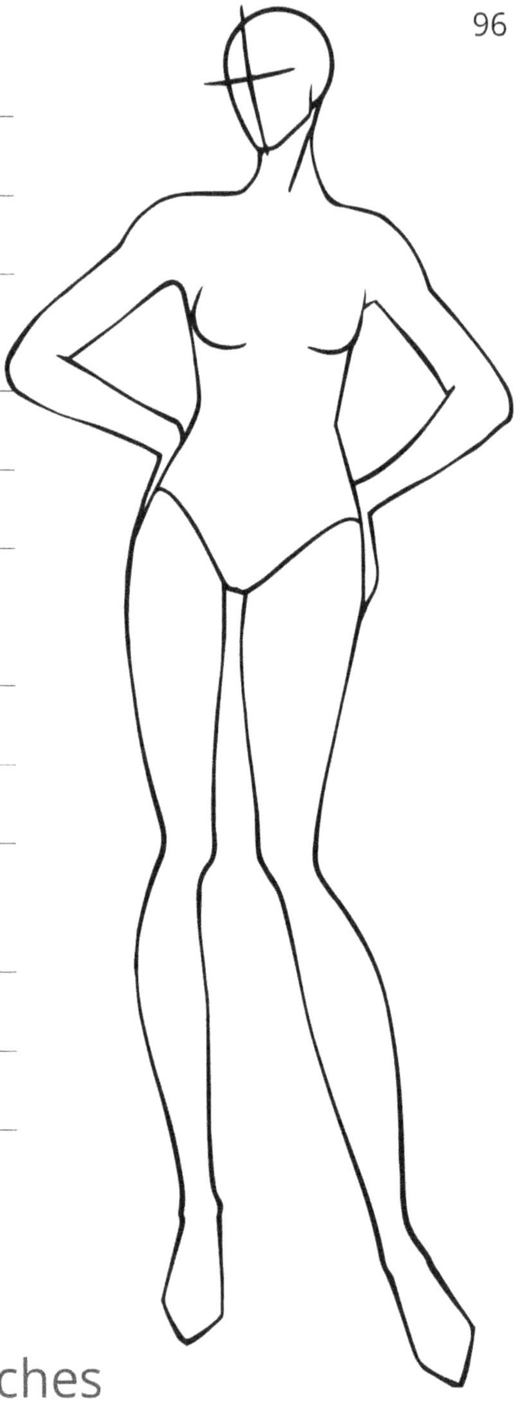

Trends

Inspiration

Textiles

Notes

Details

Swatches

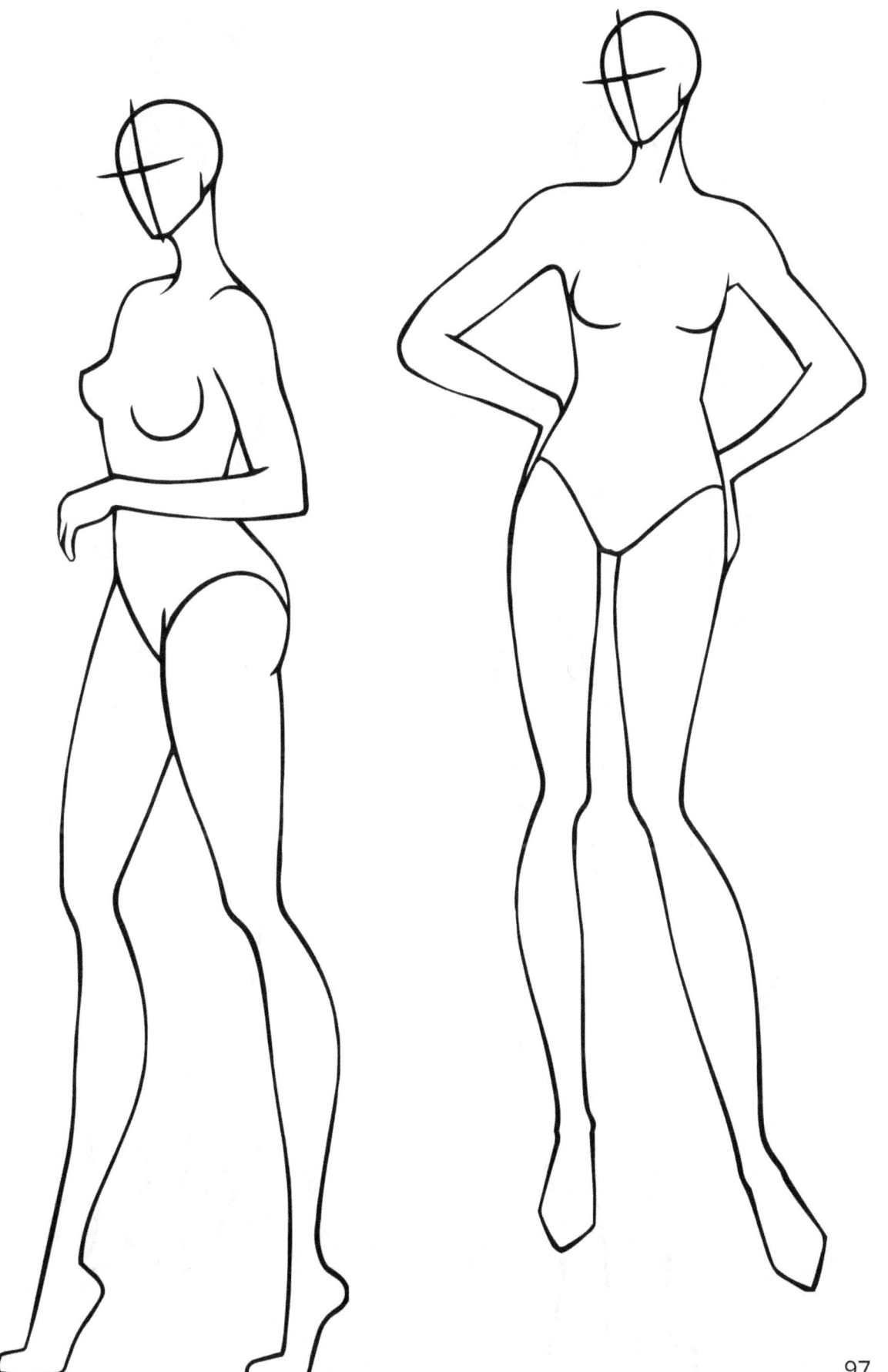

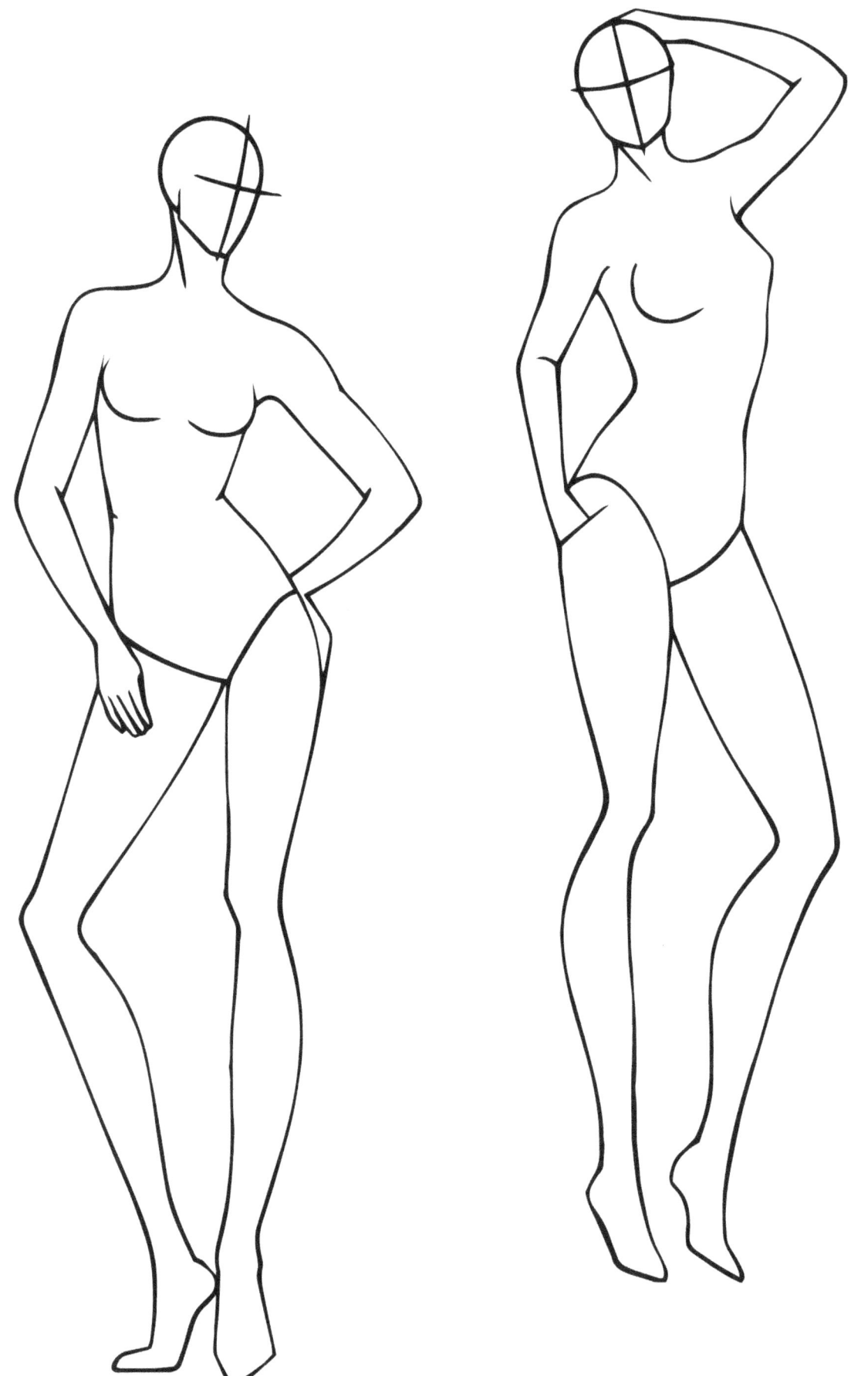

Your Notes & Inspiration Photos

This page is your creative gallery. Use it to track your progress, capture your favorite designs, and reflect on your journey.

- Add sketches, inspiration photos, or cutouts to bring your fashion ideas to life.
- Write down details such as colors, fabrics, or outfit elements that inspired you.
- Leave space for your future self to revisit and compare how your style evolves.

Pro Tip: *A single image or swatch can spark a whole collection. Don't be afraid to save even the smallest details that inspire you.*

Outfit Inspiration: Classroom Chic & Eco-Glam Couture

Classroom Chic Inspiration

A simple dress can be your go-to! Try a knee-length dress in a solid pastel, layered with a cropped jacket or cardigan. Choose breathable fabrics like cotton or linen. Add a slim belt and neutral shoes for a soft, smart look.

Eco-Glam Couture Inspiration

Eco-glam is about caring for the planet and looking amazing. Think gowns or two-piece looks made from sustainable or recycled materials- like organic cotton, bamboo fabric, or repurposed denim. Hand-painted or patchwork details make it extra special.

Pro Tip:

Being sustainable is always in style.

Fashion Practice Guide & Notes

Great designers think in collections, not just single looks.

How to Use This Page:
- Sketch 2–3 designs that belong to the same theme.
- Keep one detail consistent-like color or silhouette.
- Add notes on how each piece fits into a mini collection.

Reflection & Notes:
- Do my designs look like they belong together?
- Which outfit stands out the most?
- What ties the collection together?

Pro Tip: *Every collection tells a story-make sure yours has a theme.*

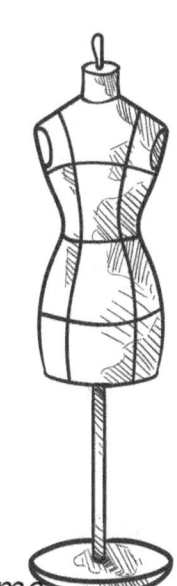

Outfit Inspiration: Streetwear

Sneakers First: Build from the Bottom Up

In streetwear, sneakers are the star. Sometimes the entire outfit is designed around them!

Pick a bold pair-chunky soles, neon details, or high-tops-and build your outfit to match.

Maybe cargo joggers tucked into socks, a cropped hoodie, and a cool jacket.

Fabric tip: Mix neutral clothes with bright shoes, or repeat a color detail from the sneakers in your accessories.

Pro Tip: *When your shoes have personality, keep the rest balanced-but never boring.*

Trends

Inspiration

Textiles

Notes

Details

Swatches

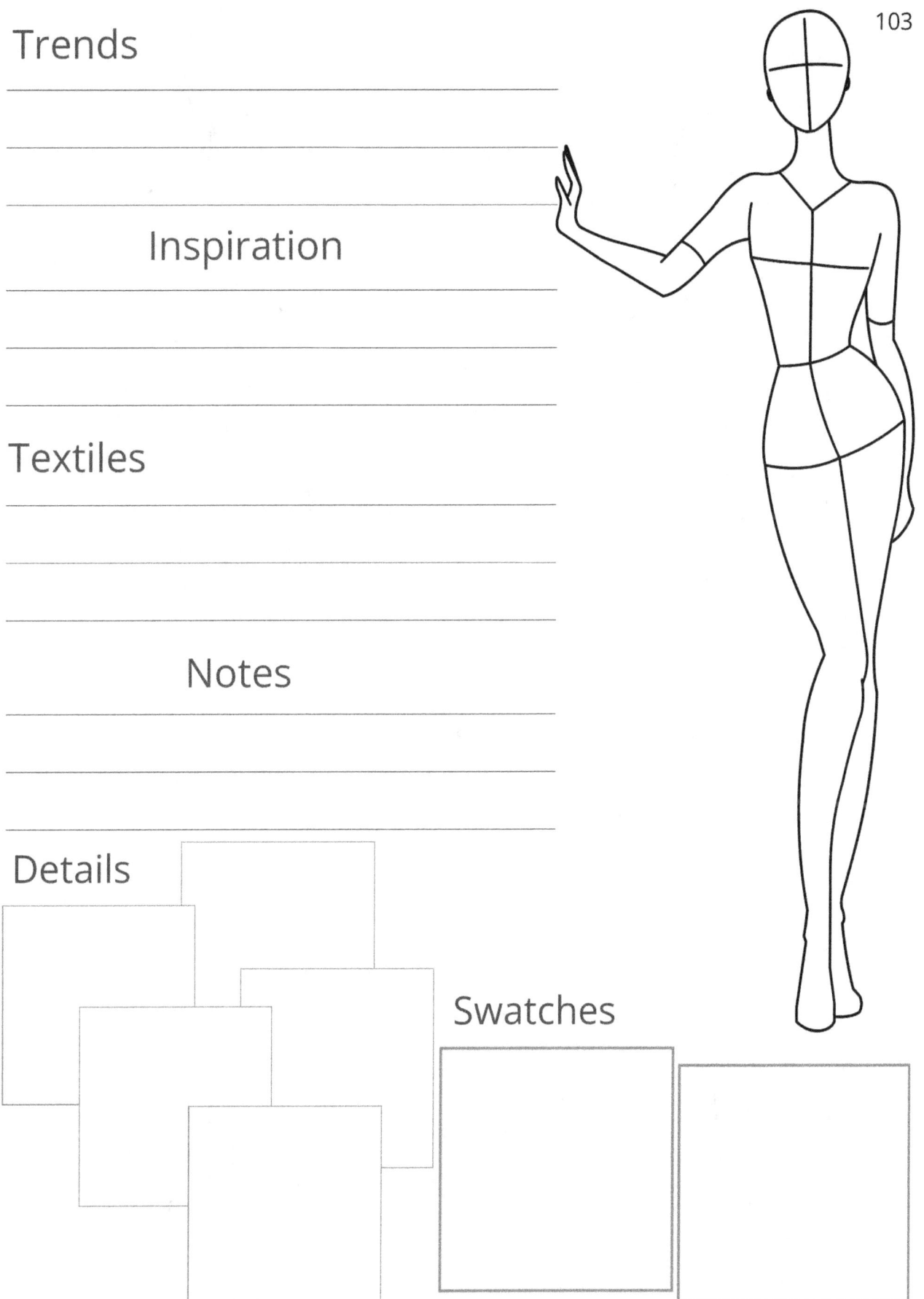

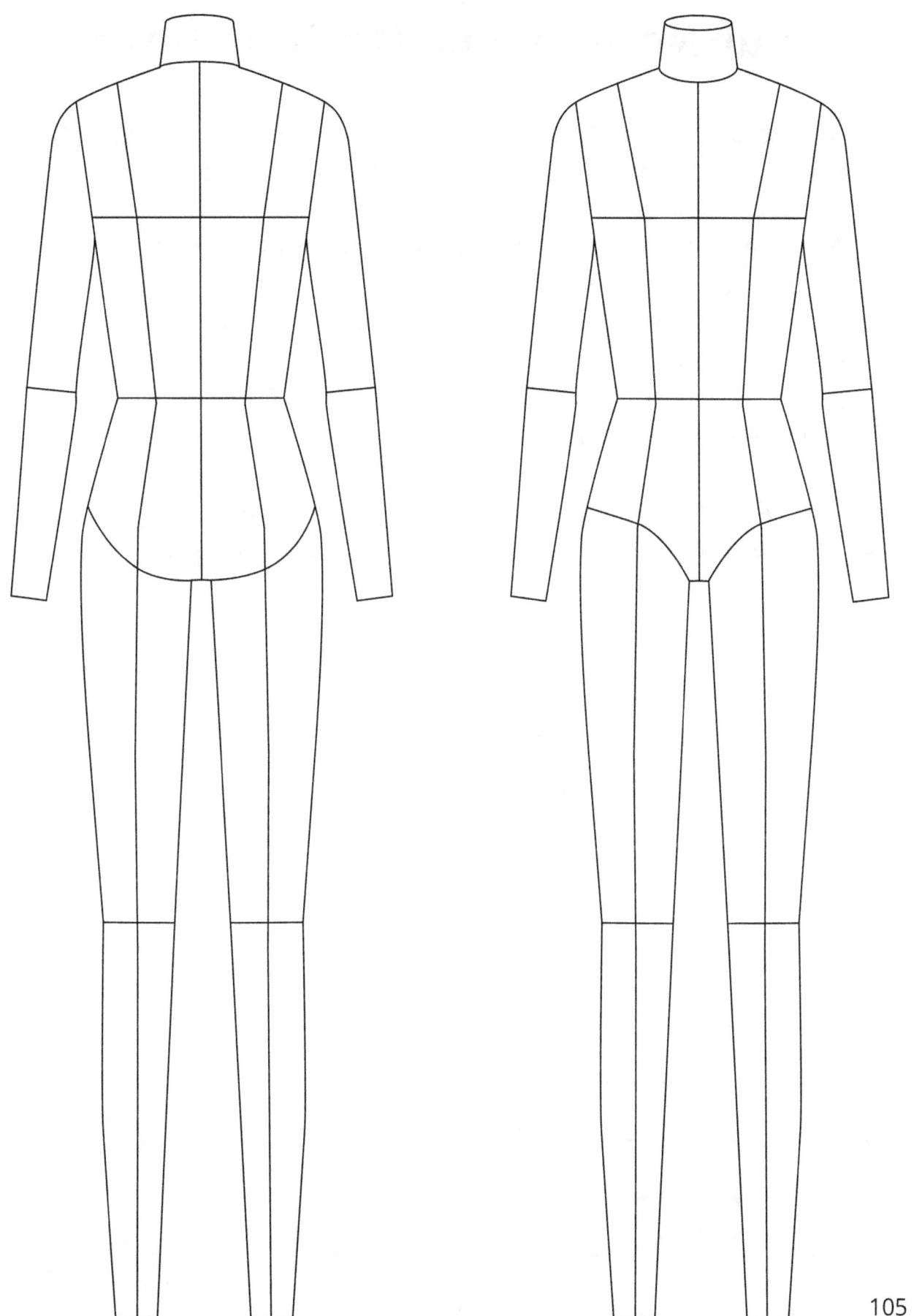

Your Notes & Inspiration Photos

This page is your creative gallery. Use it to track your progress, capture your favorite designs, and reflect on your journey.

- Add sketches, inspiration photos, or cutouts to bring your fashion ideas to life.
- Write down details such as colors, fabrics, or outfit elements that inspired you.
- Leave space for your future self to revisit and compare how your style evolves.

Pro Tip: *A single image or swatch can spark a whole collection. Don't be afraid to save even the smallest details that inspire you.*

Outfit Inspiration:
Trendy School Style & Futuristic Showstopper

Trendy School Style Inspiration

Stay current with subtle trends that fit everyday life. Oversized blazers, pastel tones, or wide-leg trousers can look professional and relaxed. Add a structured bag or platform loafers to make it modern but wearable.

Futuristic Showstopper Inspiration

Imagine a runway look that glows! Reflective fabrics, LED accents, or sculptural sleeves push creativity to the limit. This kind of look turns heads and shows fearless imagination.

Pro Tip: *Be bold-future fashion starts with your sketchbook.*

Fashion Practice Guide & Notes

Minimalism is powerful. Let your design breathe.

How to Use This Page:
- Create a look using only 3 main details.
- Focus on shape and space.
- Note how it feels without extra decoration.

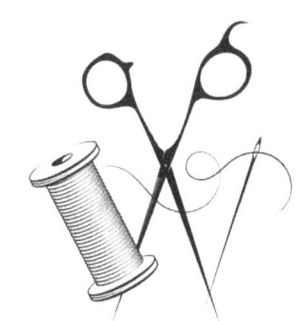

Reflection & Notes:
- Does simplicity make it stronger?
- What's the hero element here?
- What could I remove or refine?

Pro Tip: *Simplicity highlights your design skills-let your lines do the talking.*

_____
_____
_____
_____
_____
_____
_____
_____
_____

Outfit Inspiration: Streetwear

Accessories That Pop!

Accessories are everything in streetwear-they add attitude! Try beanies, chunky chains, oversized sunglasses, or crossbody mini bags.

Sketch Challenge: Draw a plain outfit and level it up with 2-3 bold accessories. See how it changes the whole look!

Pro Tip: *Accessories are the easiest way to try trends without redesigning the outfit.*

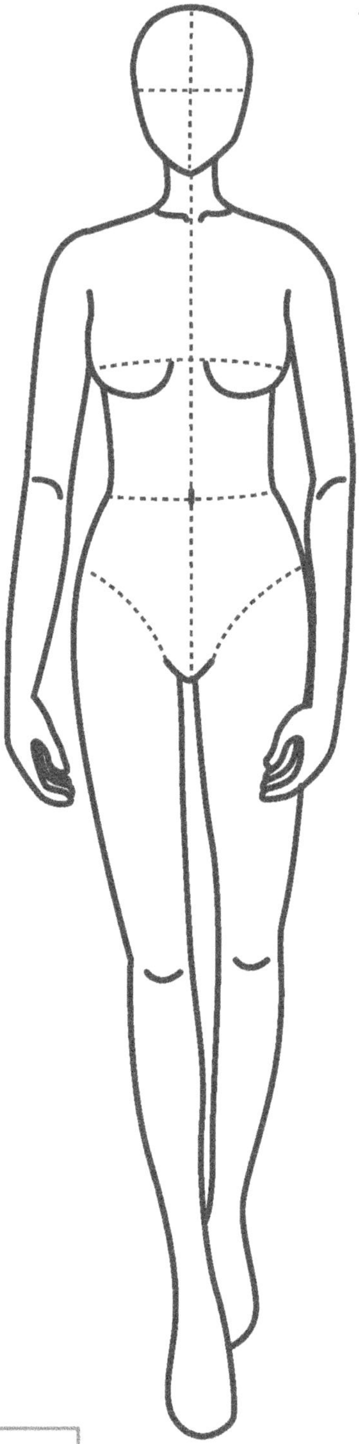

Trends

Inspiration

Textiles

Notes

Details

Swatches

110

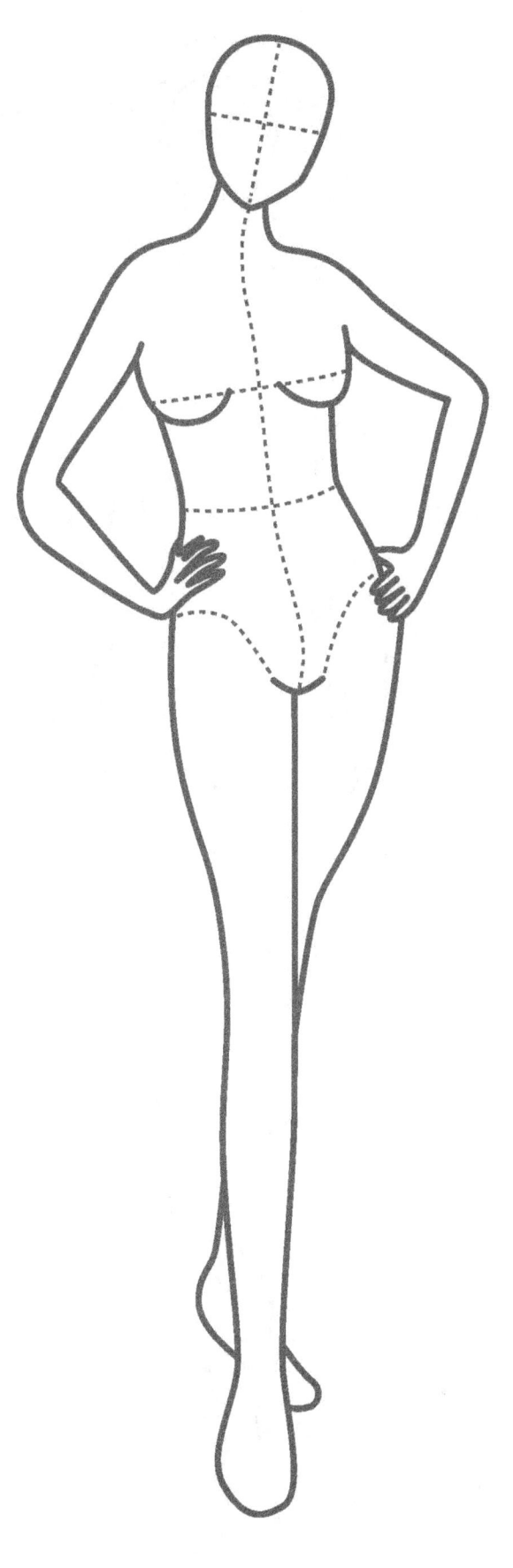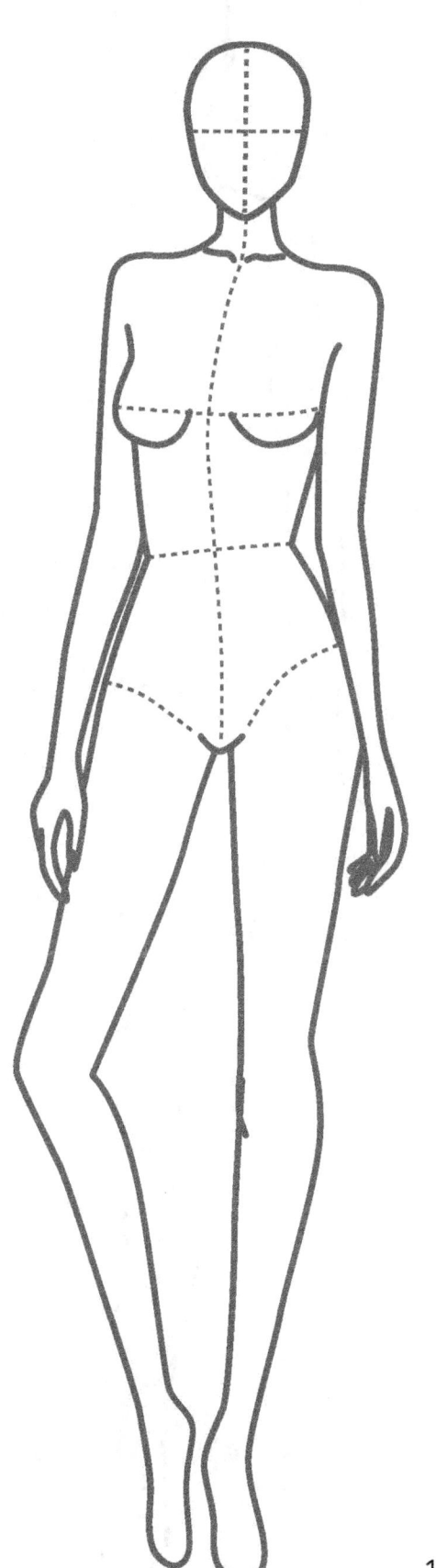

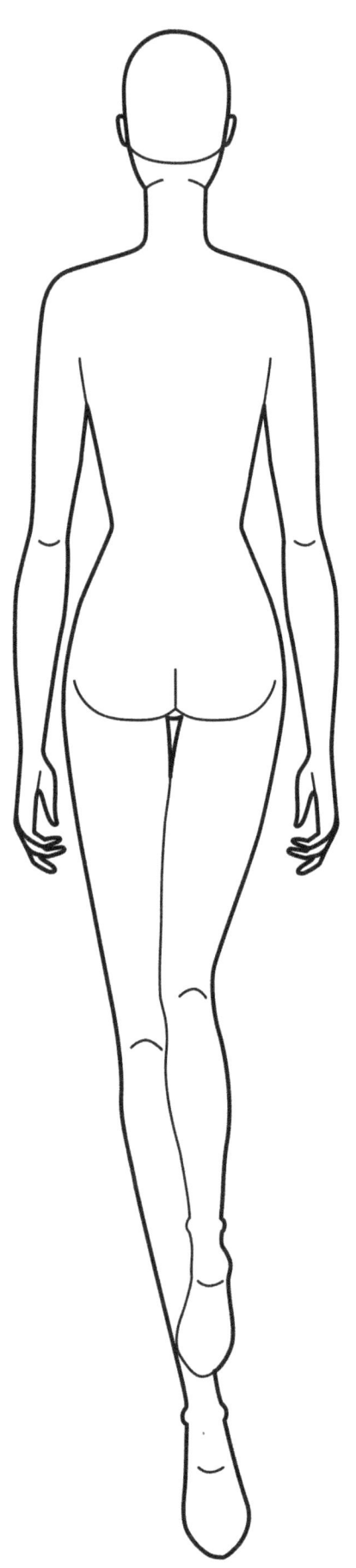
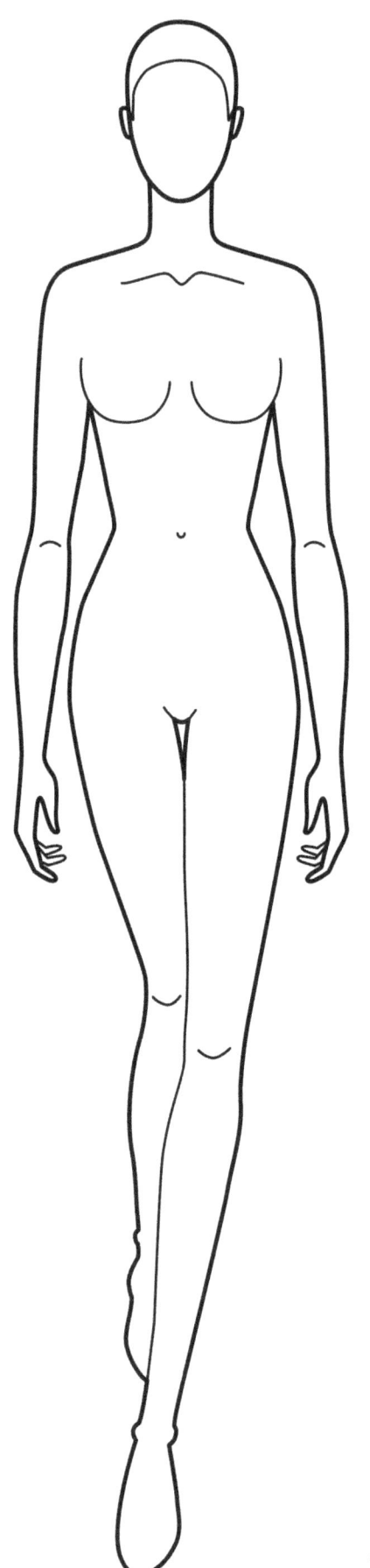

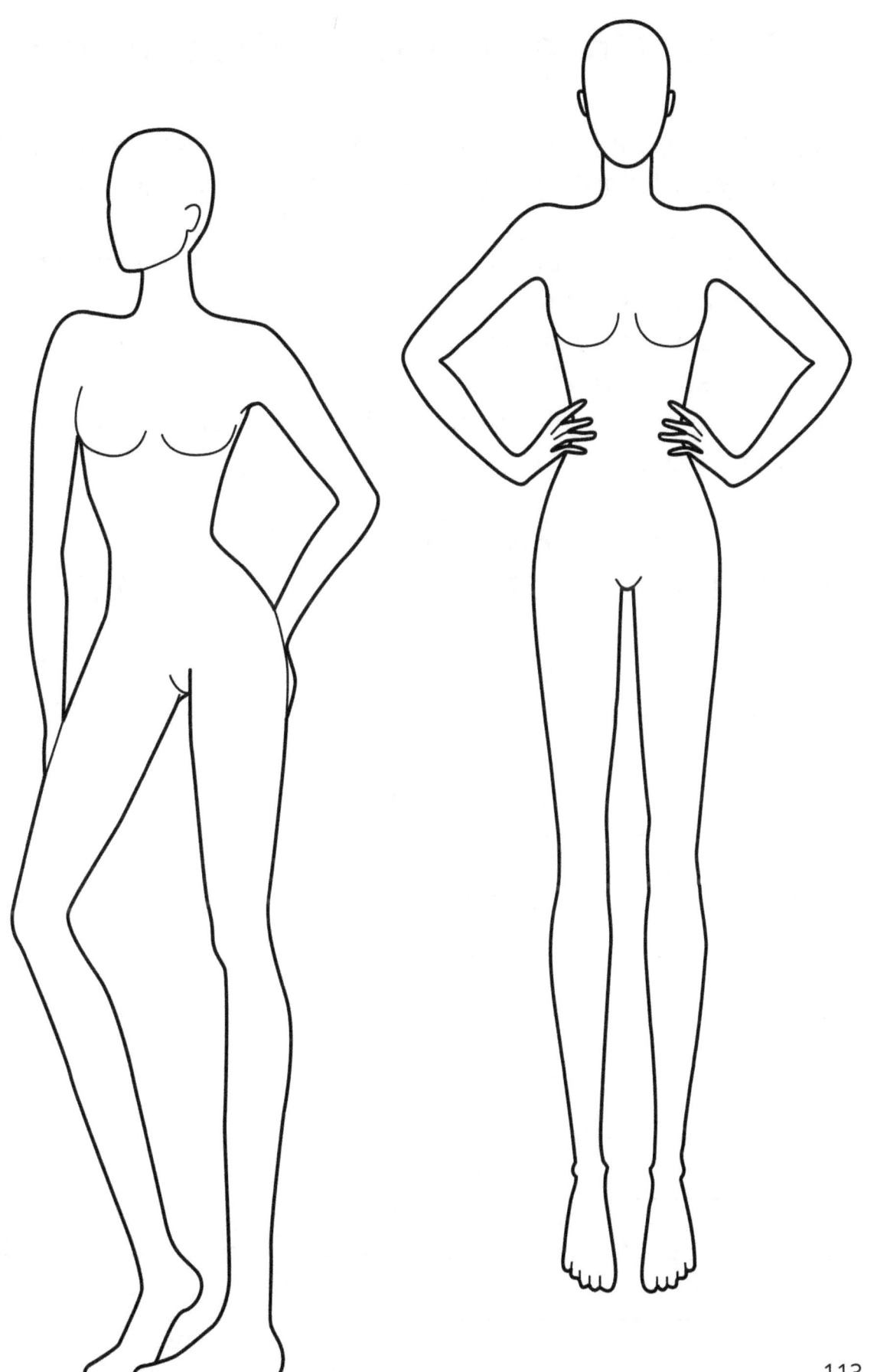

Your Notes & Inspiration Photos

This page is your creative gallery. Use it to track your progress, capture your favorite designs, and reflect on your journey.

- Add sketches, inspiration photos, or cutouts to bring your fashion ideas to life.
- Write down details such as colors, fabrics, or outfit elements that inspired you.
- Leave space for your future self to revisit and compare how your style evolves.

Pro Tip: *A single image or swatch can spark a whole collection. Don't be afraid to save even the smallest details that inspire you.*

Outfit Inspiration: Layered School Looks & Classic Glam

Layered School Look Inspiration

Layering isn't just for winter-it adds depth and style. Try a turtleneck under a slip dress, or a button-up under a jumpsuit. Add scarves, belts, or light jackets for variety. It's practical and fashion-forward.

Classic Glam Inspiration

Red carpet glam never gets old! Think sleek gowns, satin fabrics, or elegant draping. Add sparkle with statement jewelry and a confident pose. This timeless style says: "I've arrived."

Pro Tip: *Great layering makes any outfit look like it came straight off the runway.*

Fashion Practice Guide & Notes

Time to celebrate your growth! Look back at what you've created and how far you've come.

How to Use This Page:
- Sketch one outfit that shows your progress.
- Write what you've learned so far.
- Set one new fashion goal for yourself.

Reflection & Notes:
- What's my proudest improvement?
- Which skill do I want to master next?
- What's my next creative step?

Pro Tip: *Growth is stylish-every page proves you're becoming a stronger designer.*

_____
_____
_____
_____
_____
_____
_____
_____

Outfit Inspiration: Streetwear

Streetwear = Self-Expression

The best part about streetwear? It's all about you.
Mix oversized, sporty, feminine, or bold styles to tell your story. Don't follow trends-start them.

Sketch Exercise: Design an outfit that feels 100% like your vibe. Use your favorite colors, shapes, or cultural influences. Add your own logo or pattern idea.

Final Thought: Streetwear isn't just fashion-it's confidence in fabric form.

Trends

Inspiration

Textiles

Notes

Details

Swatches

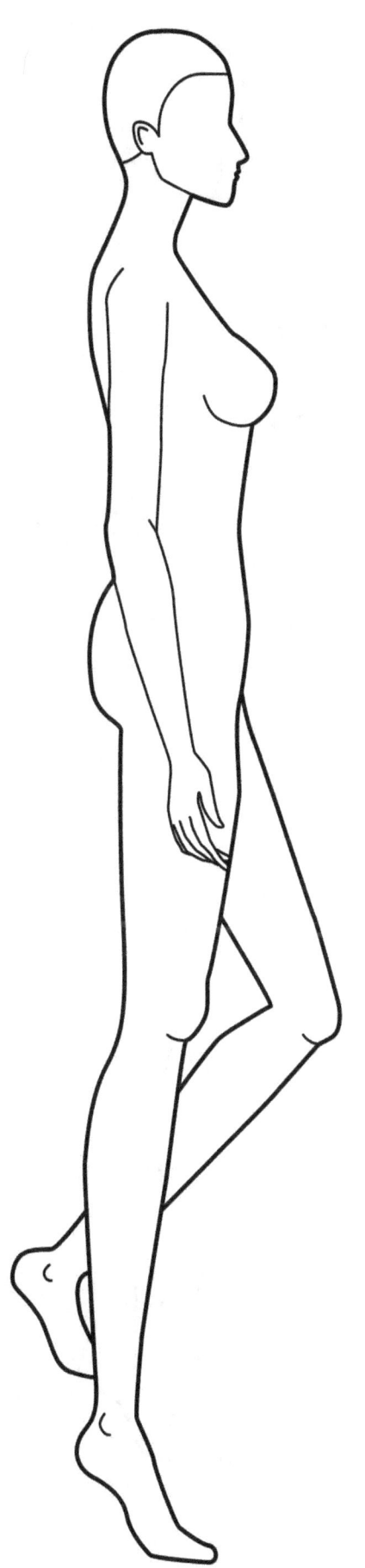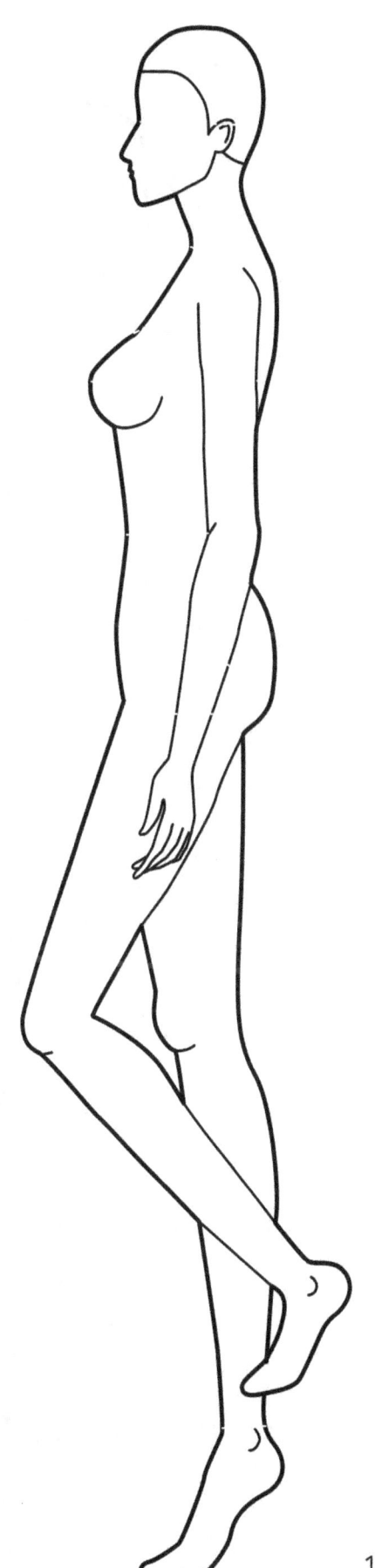

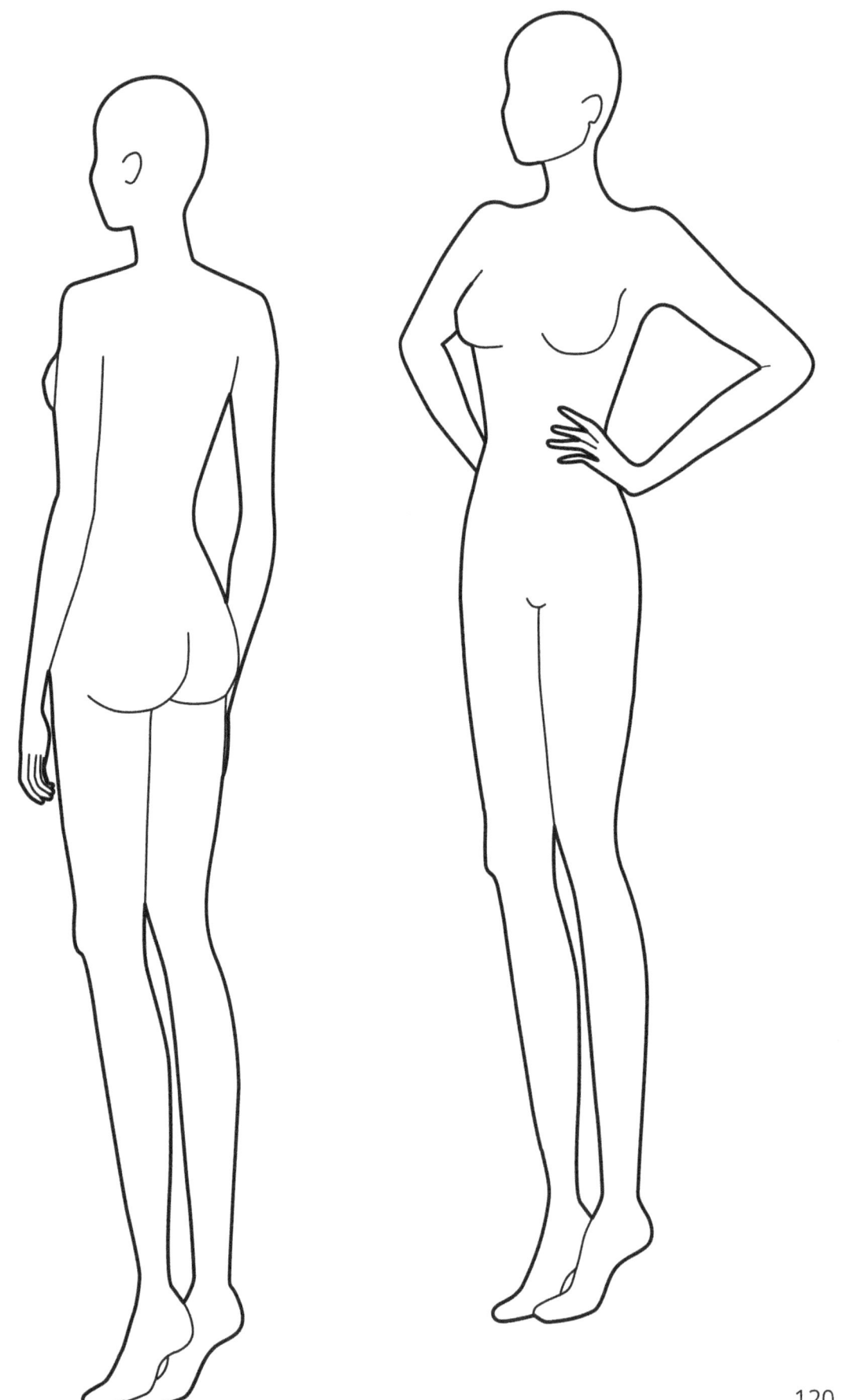

Your Notes & Inspiration Photos

This page is your creative gallery. Use it to track your progress, capture your favorite designs, and reflect on your journey.

- Add sketches, inspiration photos, or cutouts to bring your fashion ideas to life.
- Write down details such as colors, fabrics, or outfit elements that inspired you.
- Leave space for your future self to revisit and compare how your style evolves.

Pro Tip: *A single image or swatch can spark a whole collection. Don't be afraid to save even the smallest details that inspire you.*

Outfit Inspiration:
Bold School Statement & Avant-Garde Dream

Bold School Statement Inspiration

Make a confident impression with color! Try a bright suit in red, blue, or emerald green-pair it with a simple top and sneakers or boots. You'll look bold, creative, and ready to lead.

Avant-Garde Dream Inspiration

Avant-garde fashion is like wearable art. Think dramatic shapes, layered pieces, and unexpected textures. Oversized sleeves, asymmetrical cuts, or unique materials can turn your sketch into a masterpiece.

Pro Tip: *Push boundaries-fashion evolves when you take risks.*

Trends

Inspiration

Textiles

Notes

Details

Swatches

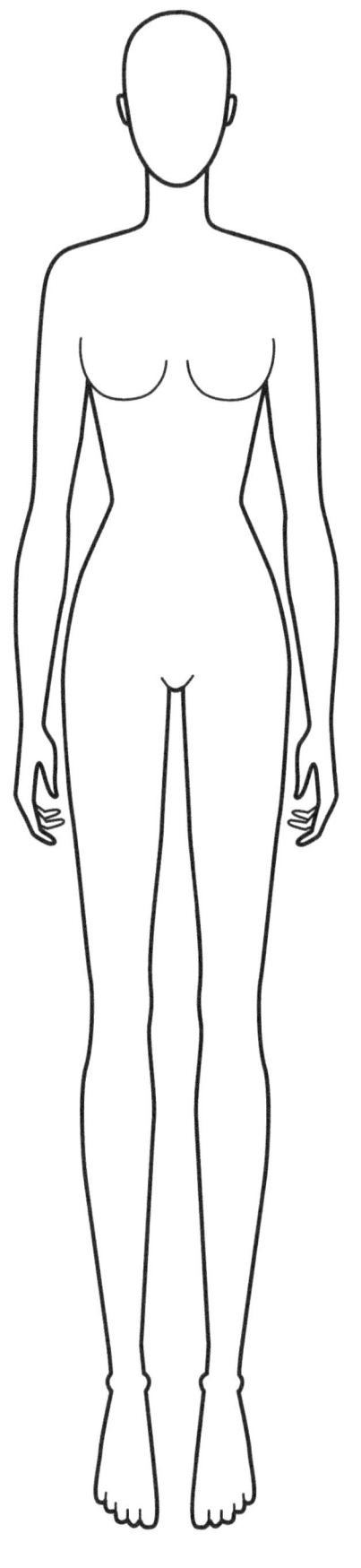

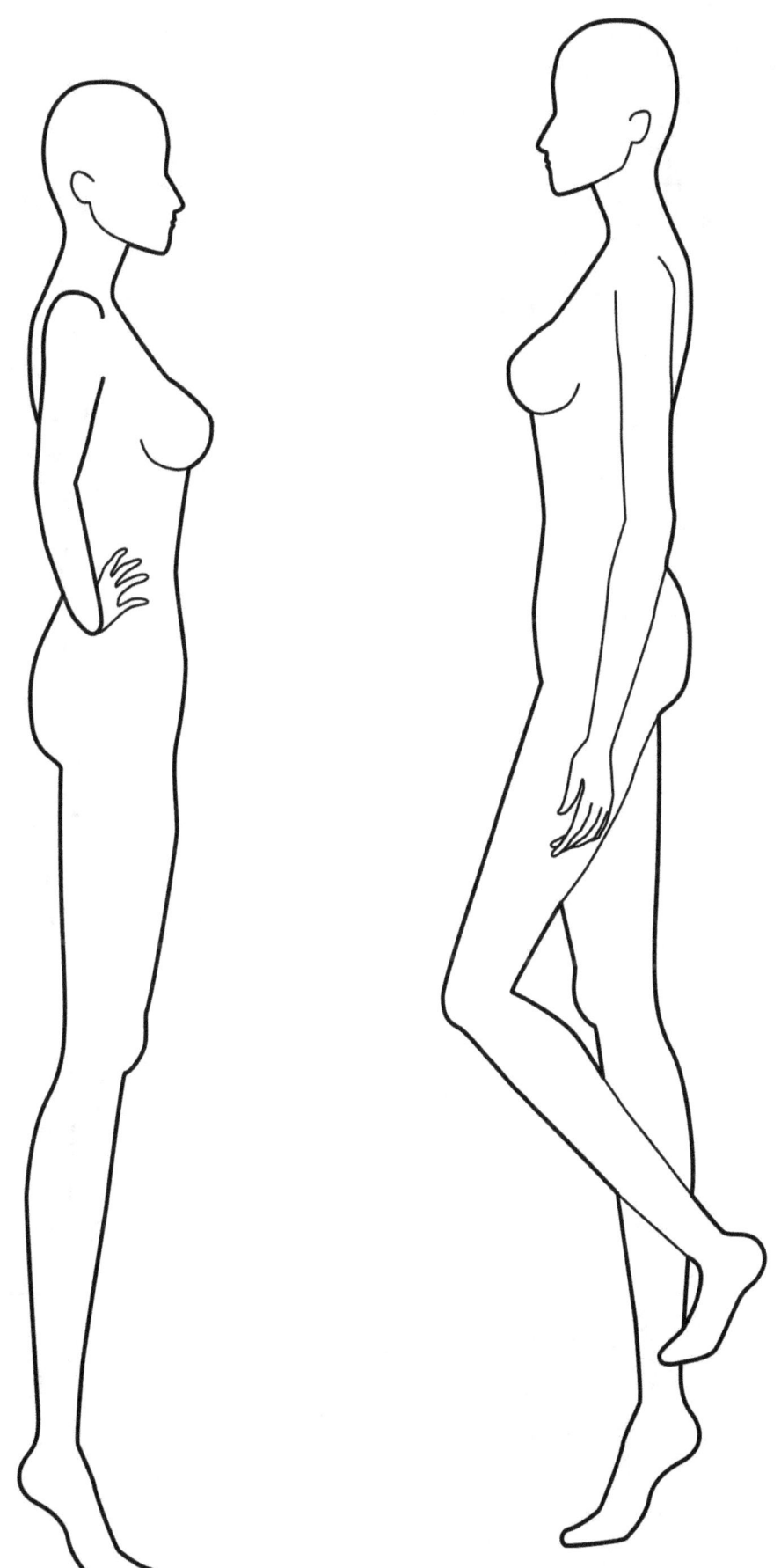

Trends

Inspiration

Textiles

Notes

Details

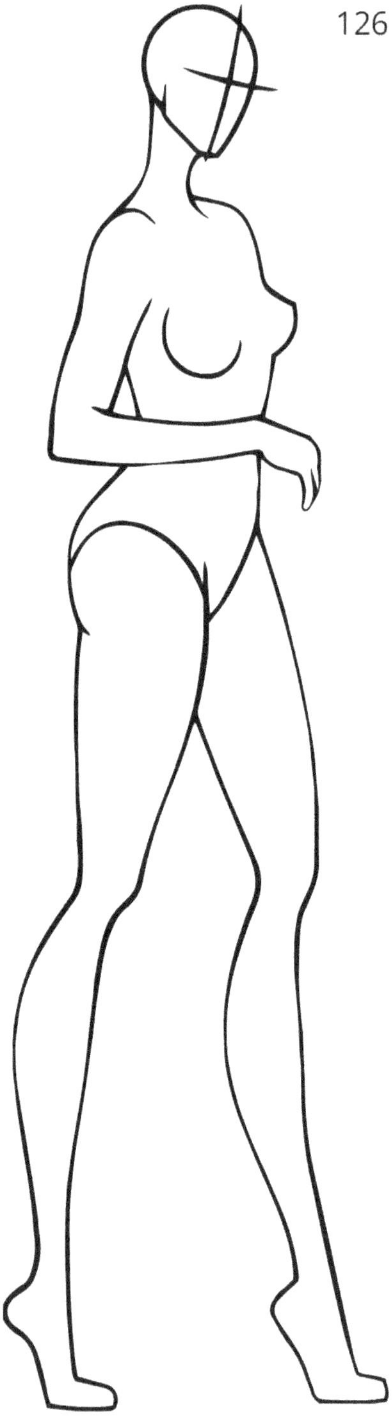

Swatches

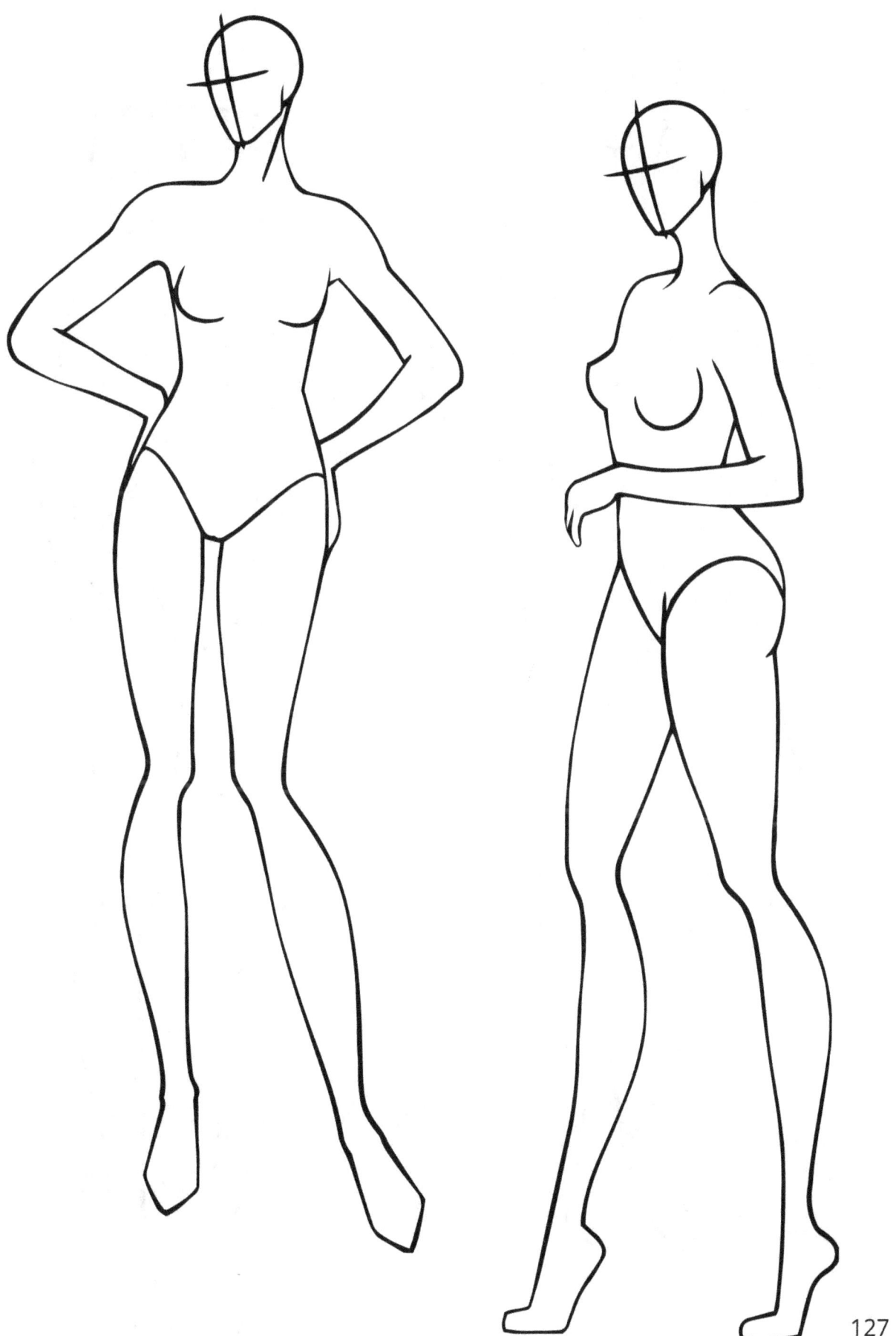

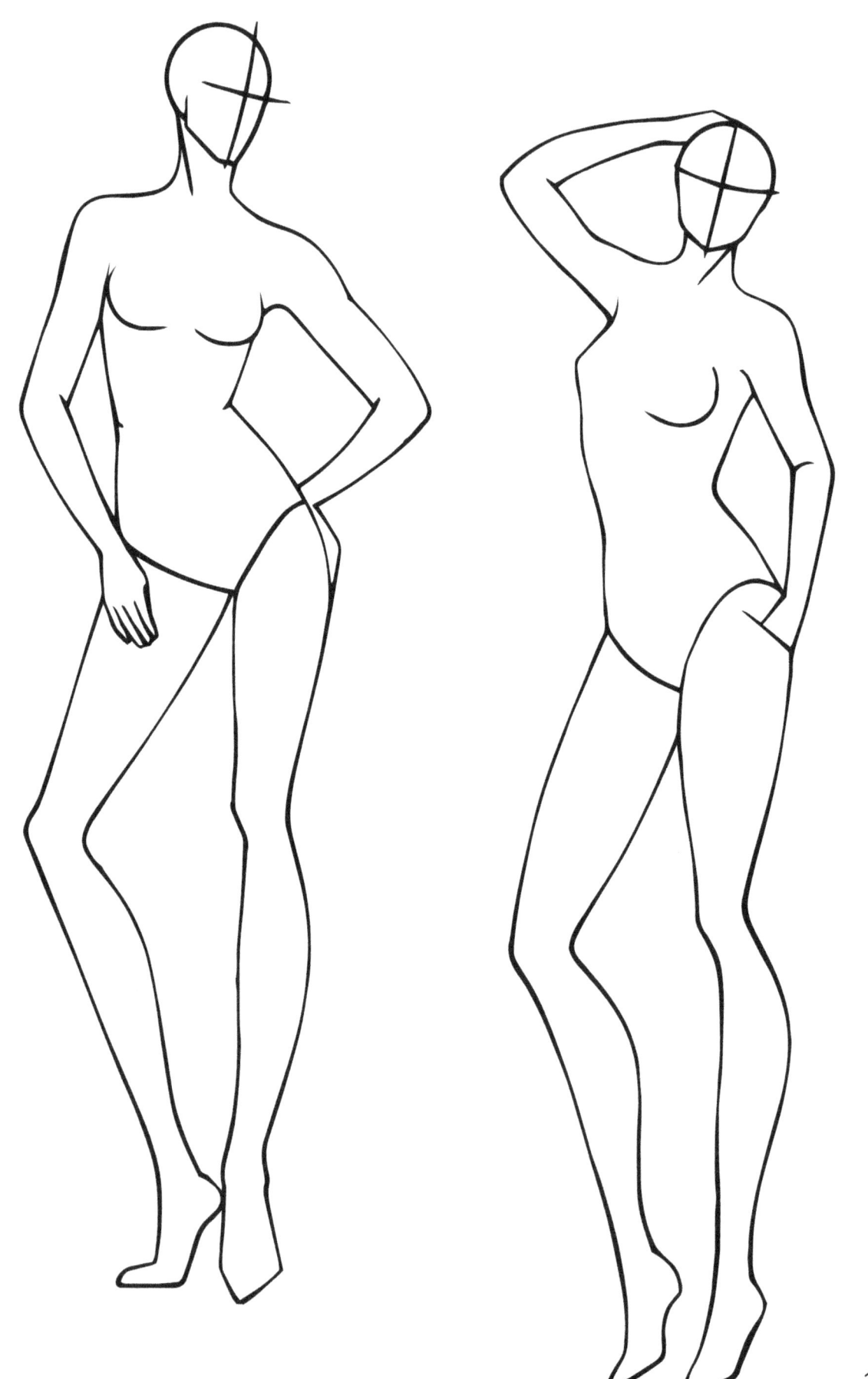

Trends

Inspiration

Textiles

Notes

Details

Swatches

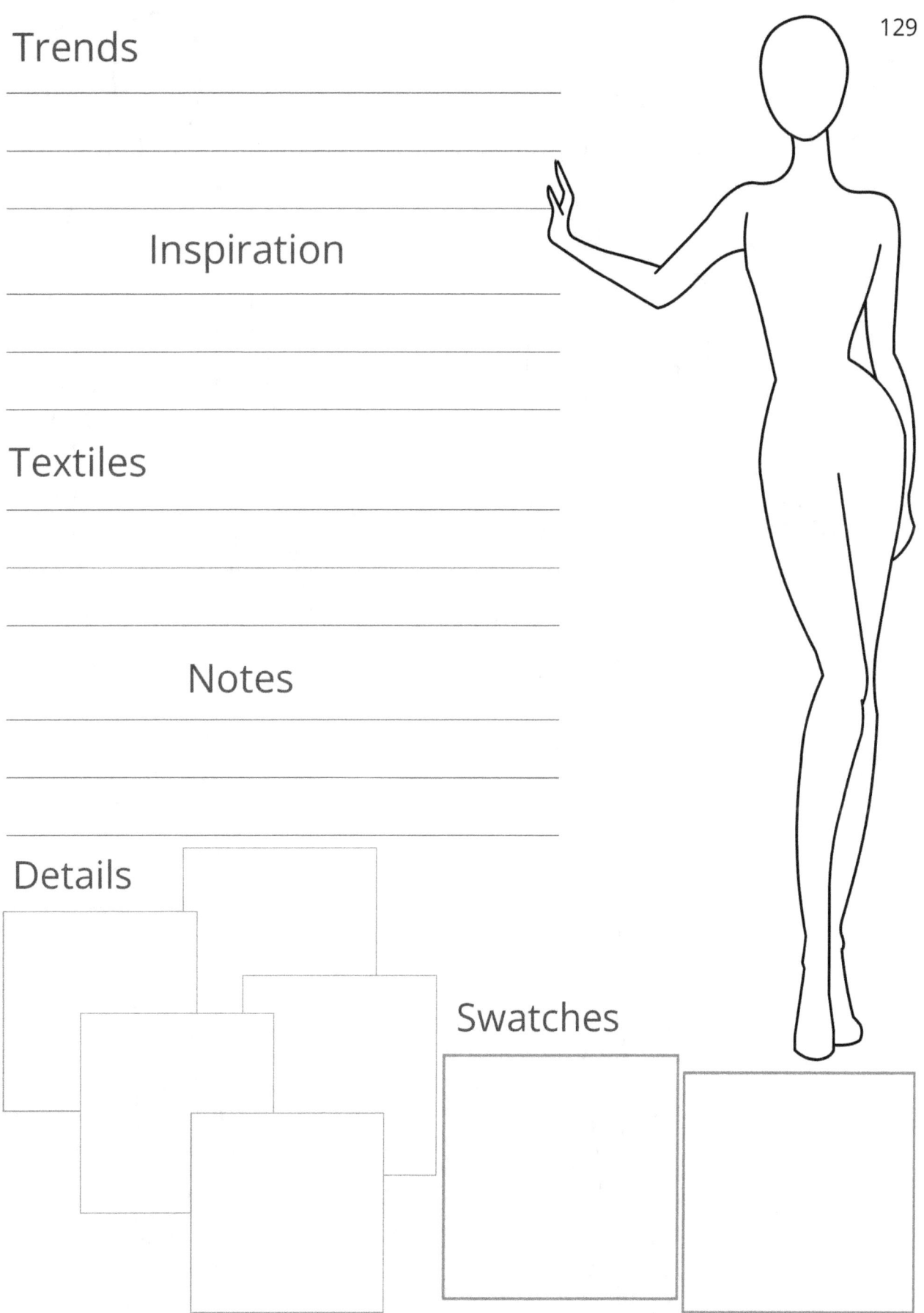

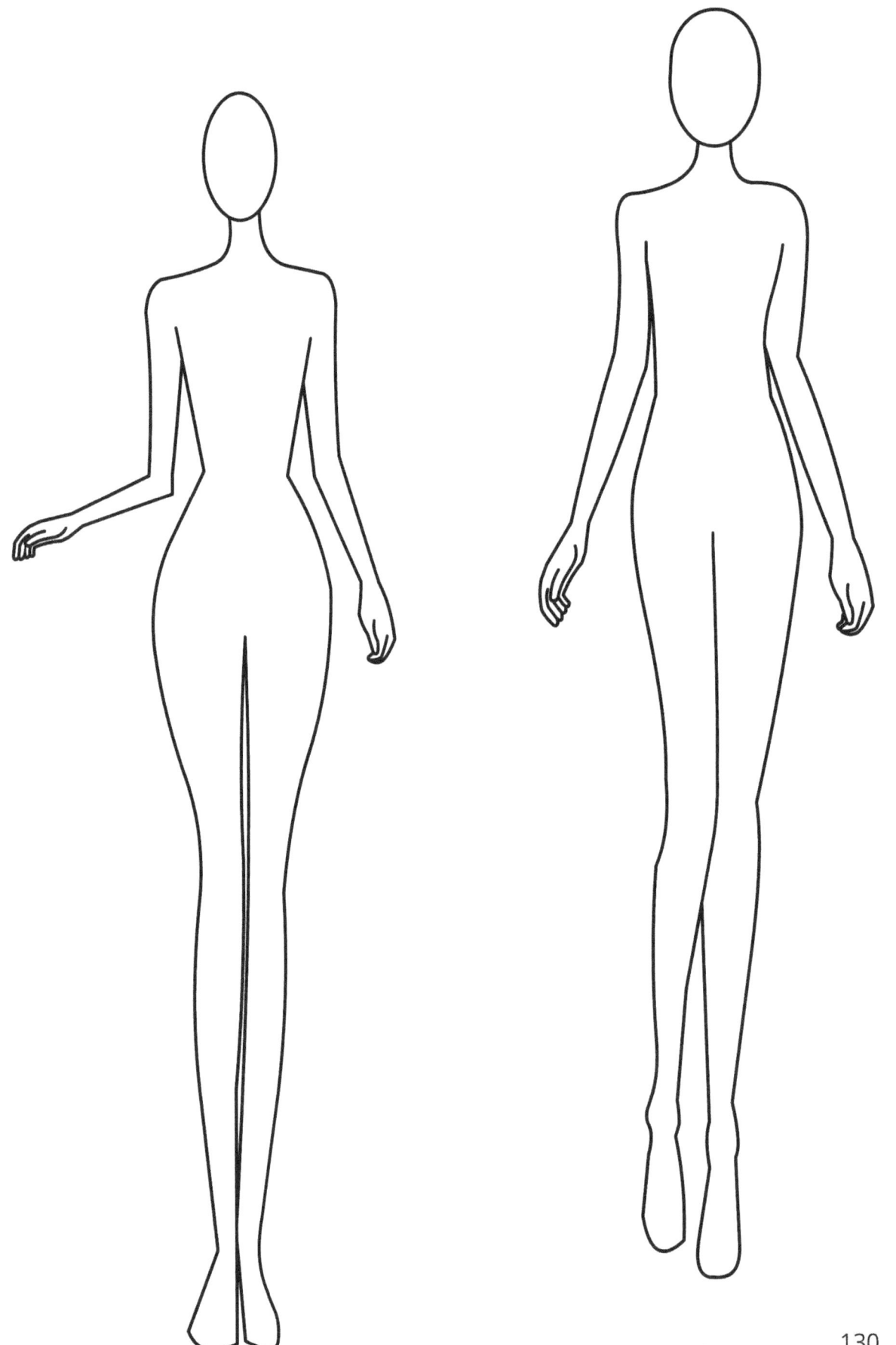

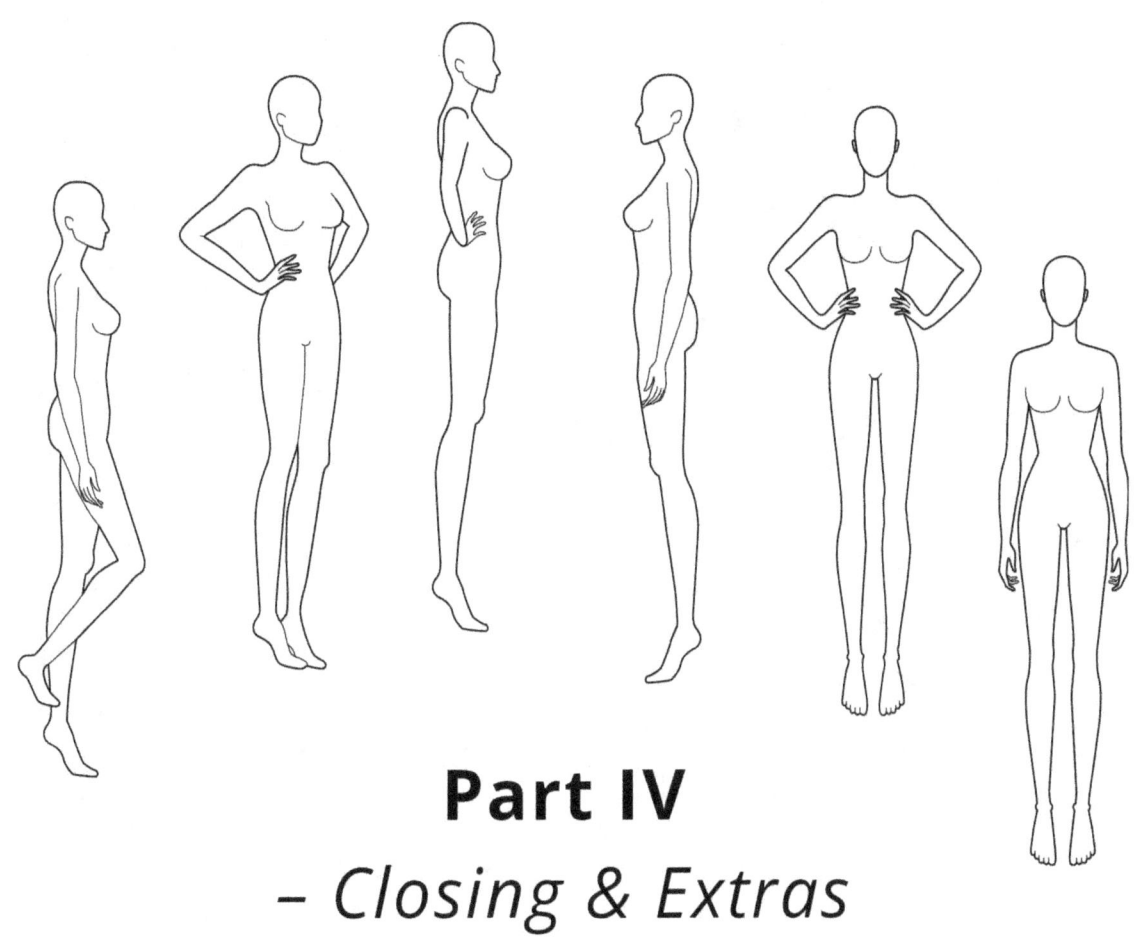

Part IV
– Closing & Extras

The Creative Wrap-Up

Welcome to the final chapter of your fashion journey!

This section is all about reflection, experimentation, and celebrating how far you've come.

You'll find fun creative challenges, design prompts, and extra spaces to keep practicing your ideas and exploring your unique style.

Remember - there's no finish line in creativity.

Every page you complete here is proof that your imagination has no limits.

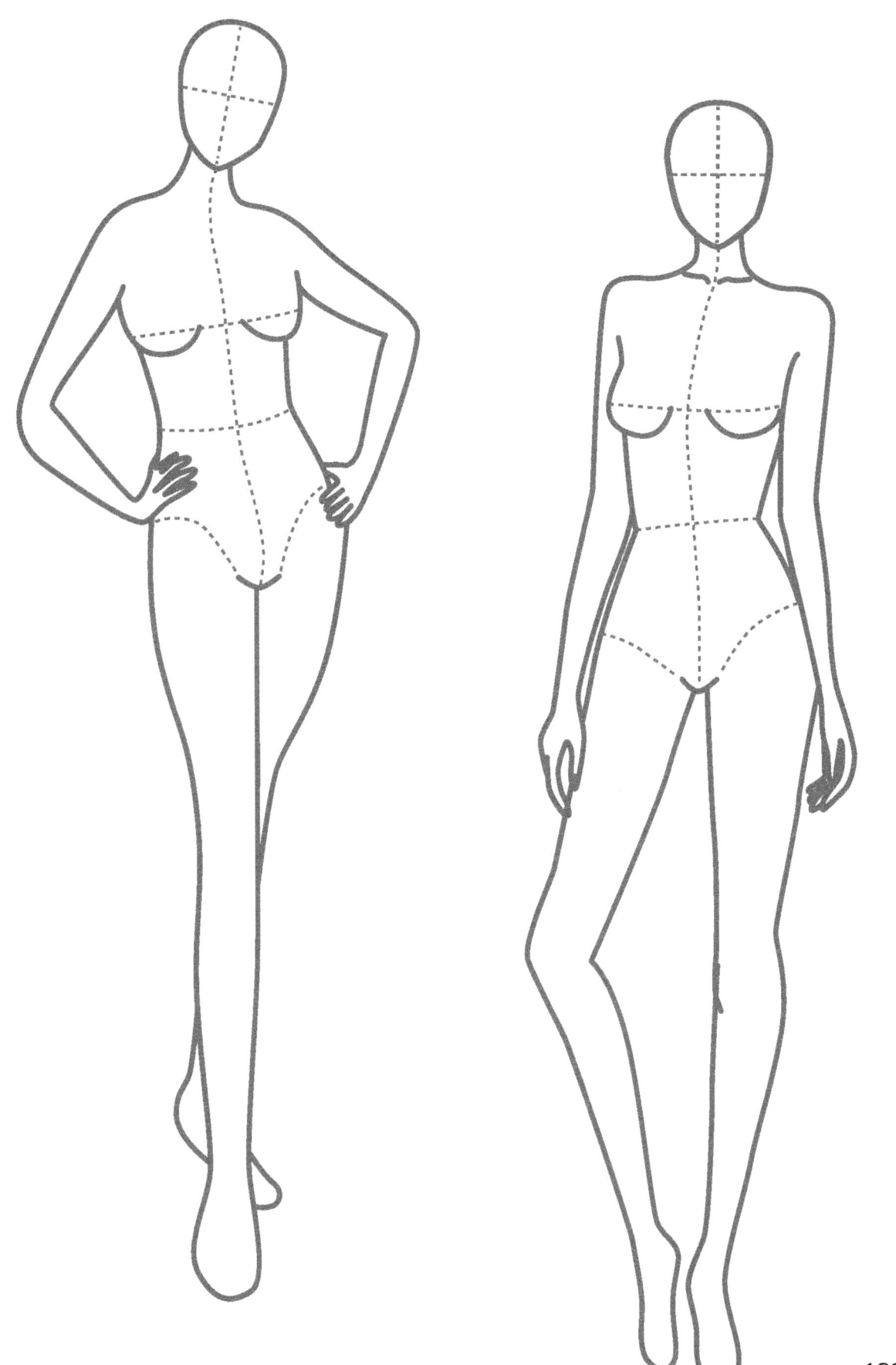

Redesign a Classic Silhouette

Take a timeless shape-like a denim jacket, trench coat, or A-line dress-and reinvent it your way! Think about how color, fabric, and details can make a classic piece feel totally new and exciting. Try adding cutouts, asymmetry, or cool stitching.

This challenge helps you learn how to refresh classics while keeping the original spirit.

Guided Prompts:
- Which classic item did you choose?
- What modern twist did you add?
- Describe your redesign in one word.

Pro Tip: *Even legends can glow up. Classic + Creativity = Timeless Cool.*

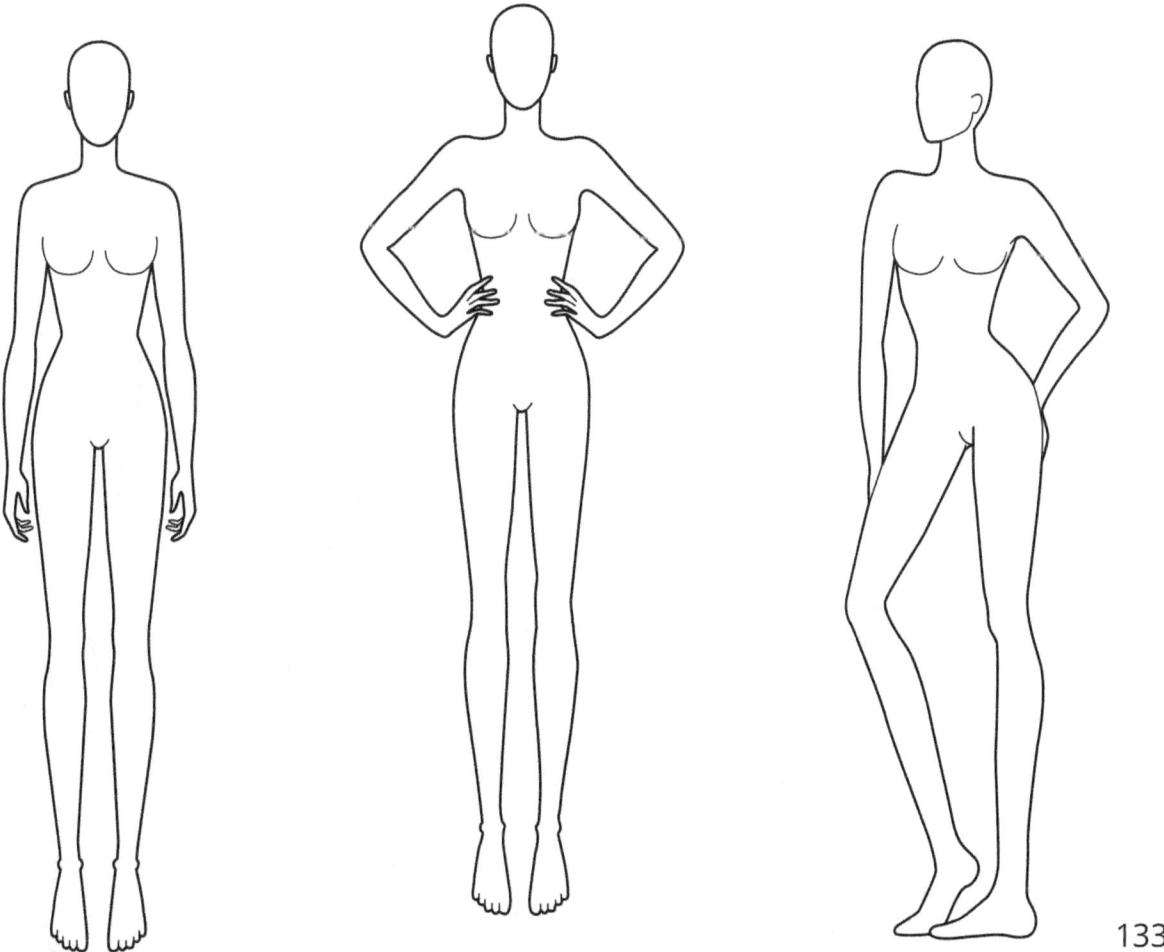

Mini Capsule Challenge

Design a 5-piece capsule wardrobe that could fit in your school locker but still show off your personality. Pick tops, bottoms, and outerwear that mix and match to create different looks.

This exercise helps you master balance, coordination, and personal style identity.

Prompts:
 • What's your capsule theme? (e.g. chill street, soft pastel, artsy edge)
 • What colors or fabrics stand out?
 • How do the pieces mix together?

Pro Tip: *When every piece works with everything else-you've created magic.*

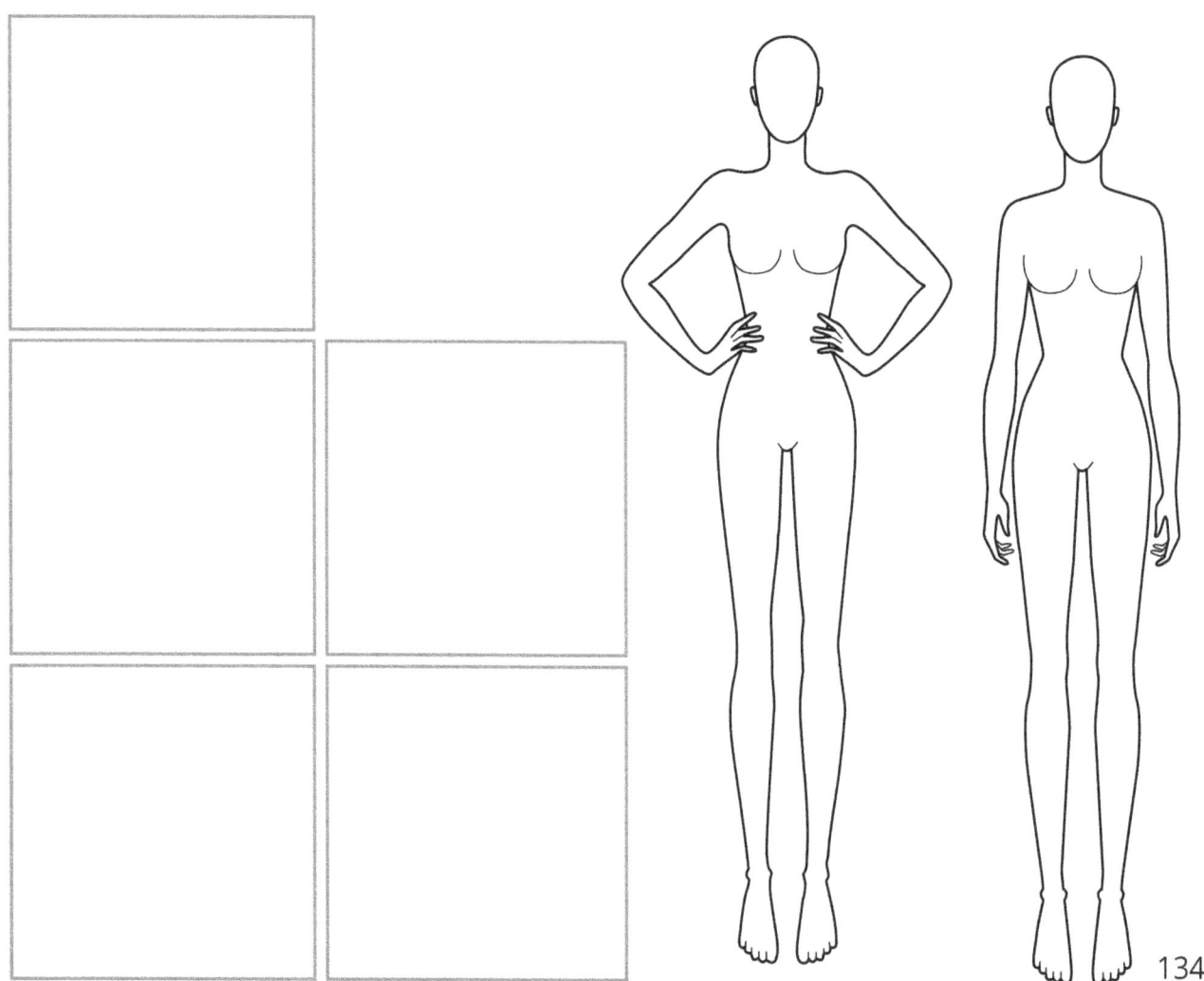

Seasonal Inspiration

Pick a season-spring, summer, fall, or winter-and design an outfit inspired by its energy. Go beyond the obvious: winter can be pink and sparkly, and summer can be soft and earthy.
 Let the season's feeling guide your design.

Prompts:
 • Which season inspired you?
 • What colors or textures capture its mood?
 • How is your take different from typical seasonal looks?

Pro Tip: Surprise people-fashion seasons are what you make them.

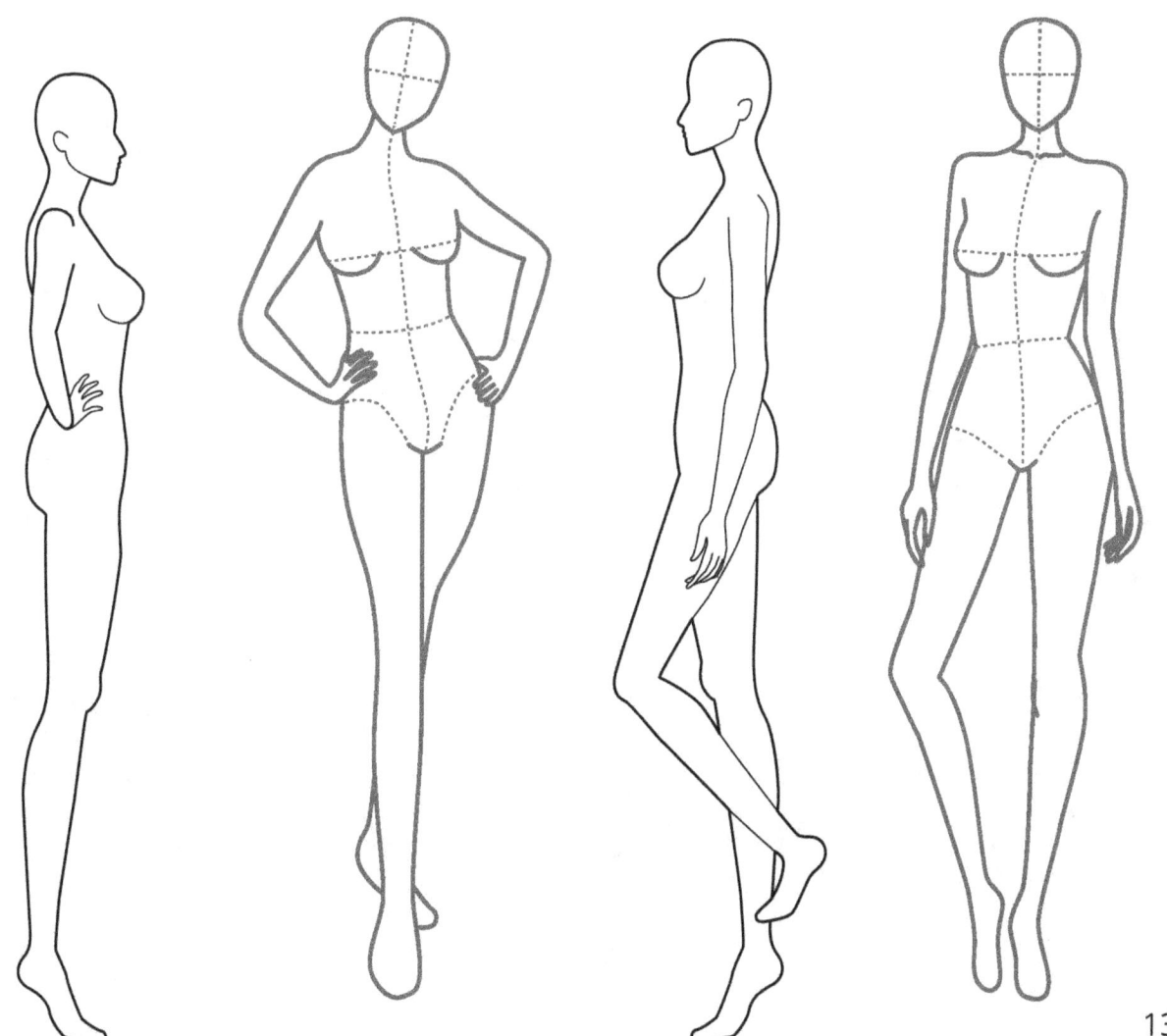

T-Shirt Glow-Up Challenge

Take the most basic thing-a plain tee-and turn it into something bold. Change the sleeves, crop it, add graphics, mix fabrics, or even turn it into a dress or hoodie.
 Keep the original shape but make it unforgettable.

Prompts:
  • What's the vibe of your new T-shirt?
  • Which detail did you change most?
  • Where would someone wear it?

Pro Tip: *Simple pieces = endless possibilities.*

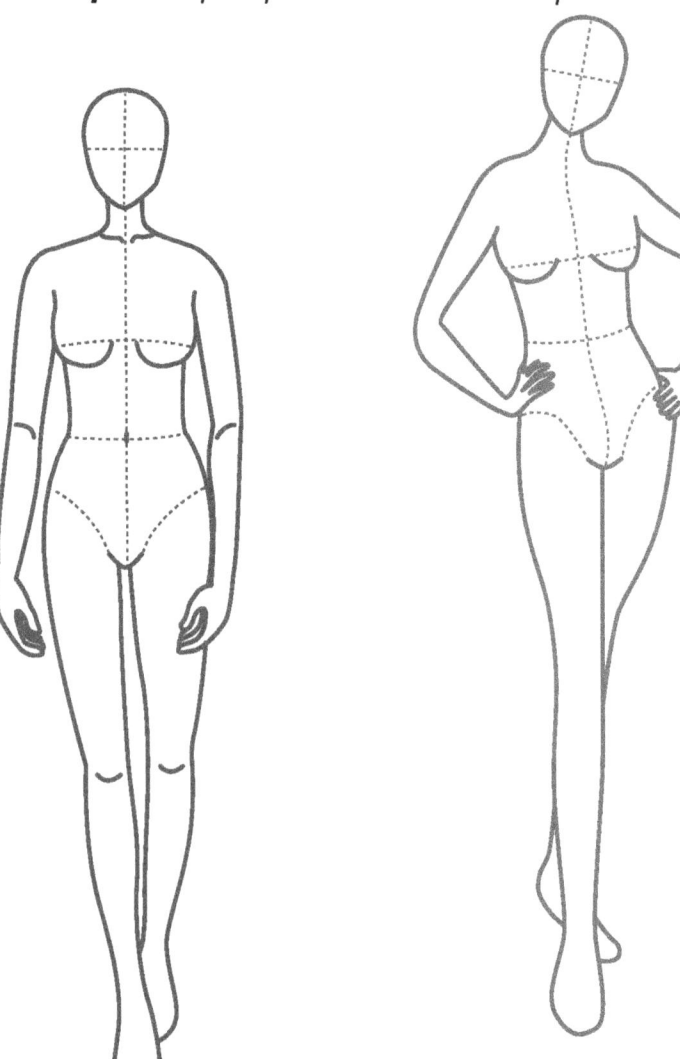
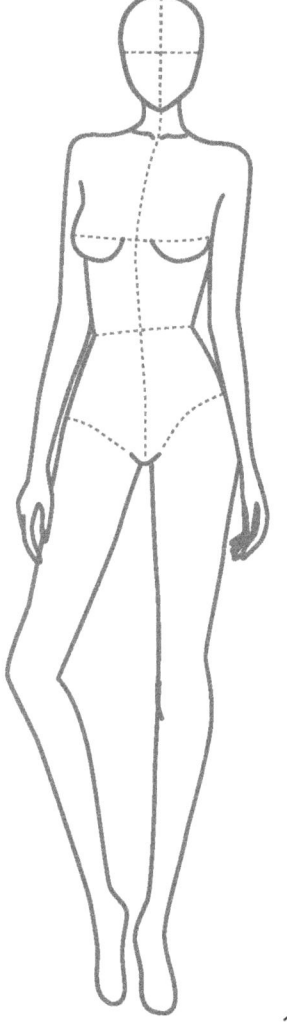

Mix & Match Opposites

Combine two styles that totally clash-like sporty + romantic, vintage + tech, or street + glam-and make them work together. This teaches you to mix unexpected ideas with confidence.

Prompts:
- Which two styles did you mix?
- What detail connects them?
- Does your look lean more to one side or feel balanced?

Pro Tip: *Contrast is where creativity lives.*

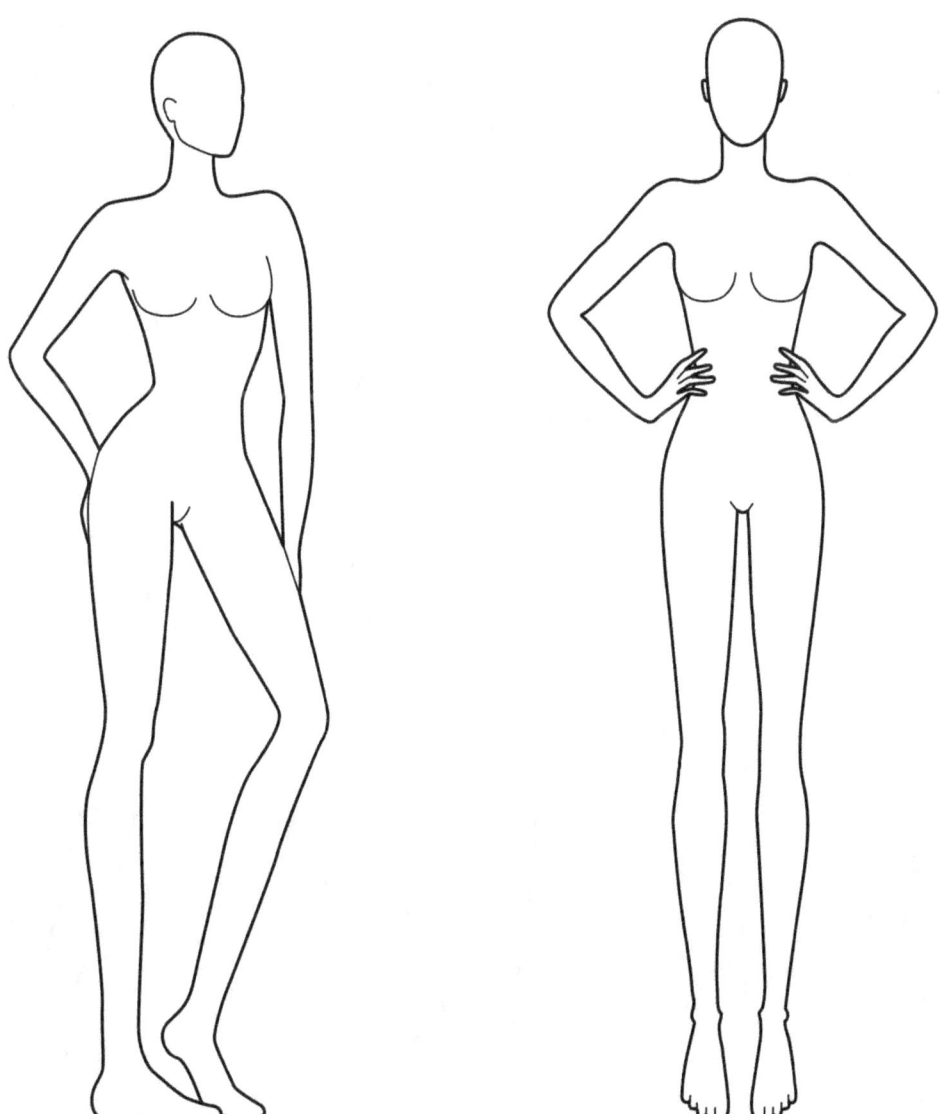

Accessory Focus

This time, accessories steal the spotlight! Hats, bags, shoes, jewelry-pick your favorites and build the outfit around them. Keep the clothes simple so the accessories pop.

Prompts:
- Which accessory is the star?
- How does your outfit support it?
- Would it still work without it?

Pro Tip: *Accessories turn "nice outfit" into "wow, that's so you."*

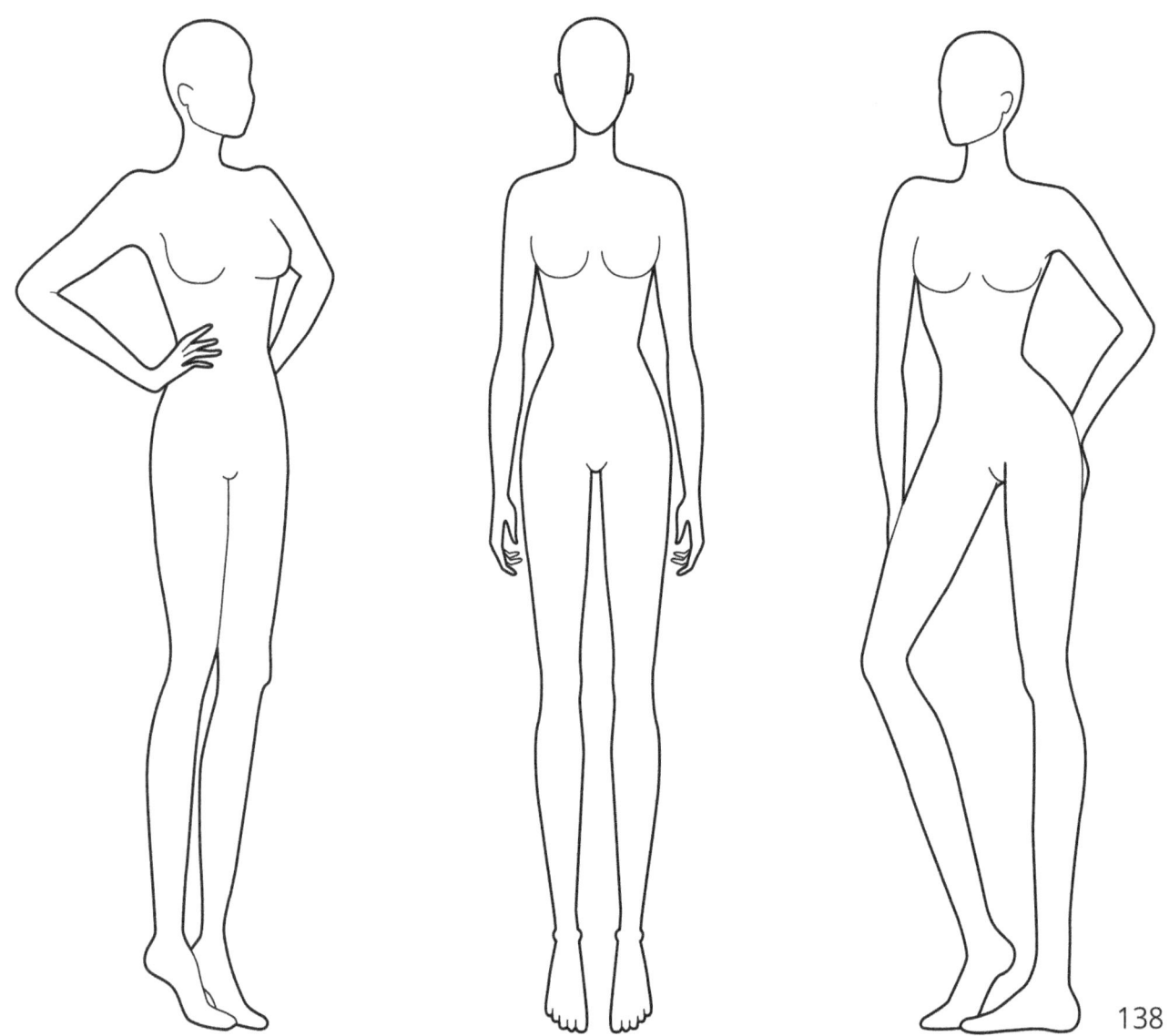

Fashion Through Time

Travel through fashion history and remix it!

Maybe 90s grunge meets Y2K sparkle, or 70s flares meet modern streetwear. Take something iconic and make it today's trend.

Prompts:
- Which decade inspired you?
- What modern twist did you add?
- How does it connect to what's trending now?

Pro Tip: Fashion always loops back-be the one who rewrites it.

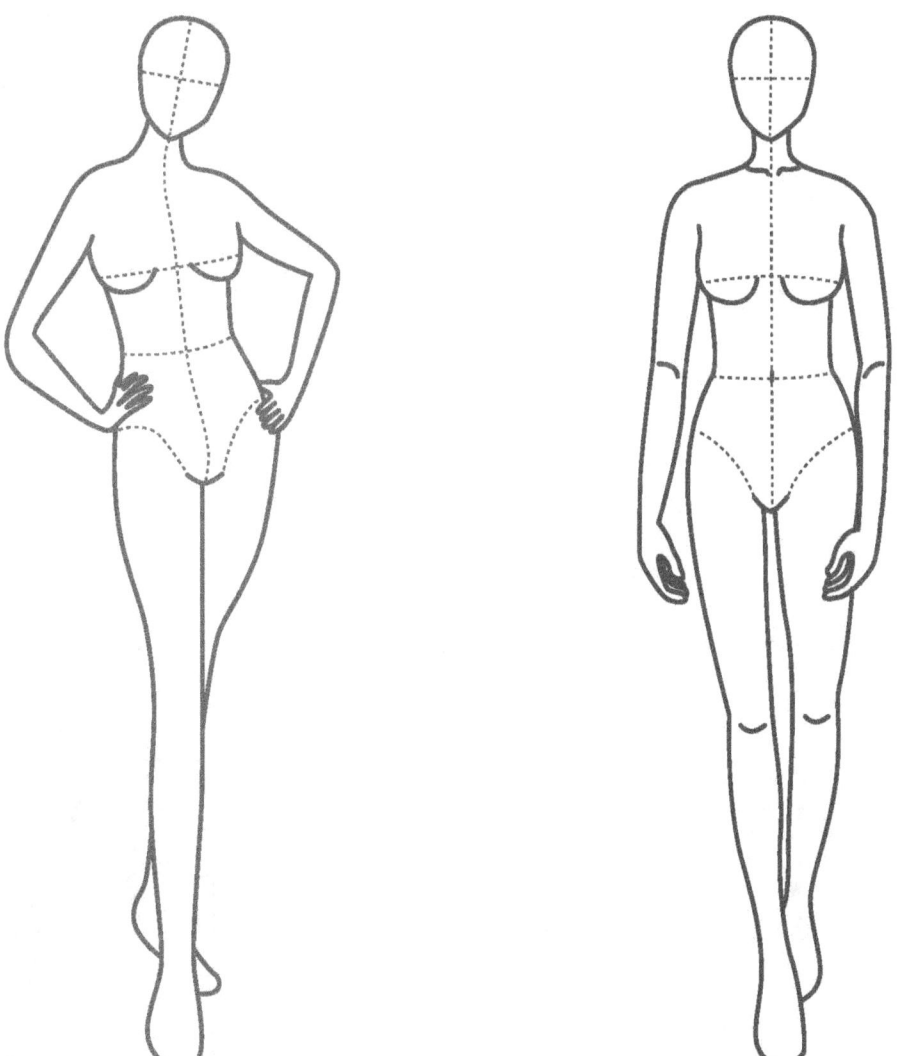

Moodboard to Outfit

Collect images, colors, and textures that inspire you, then design an outfit that matches the vibe. Paste or draw your mini moodboard first, then sketch your look next to it.

Prompts:
- What's your moodboard theme?
- Which details made it into your design?
- Does your outfit feel like your board?

Pro Tip: A clear vision makes sketching so much easier.

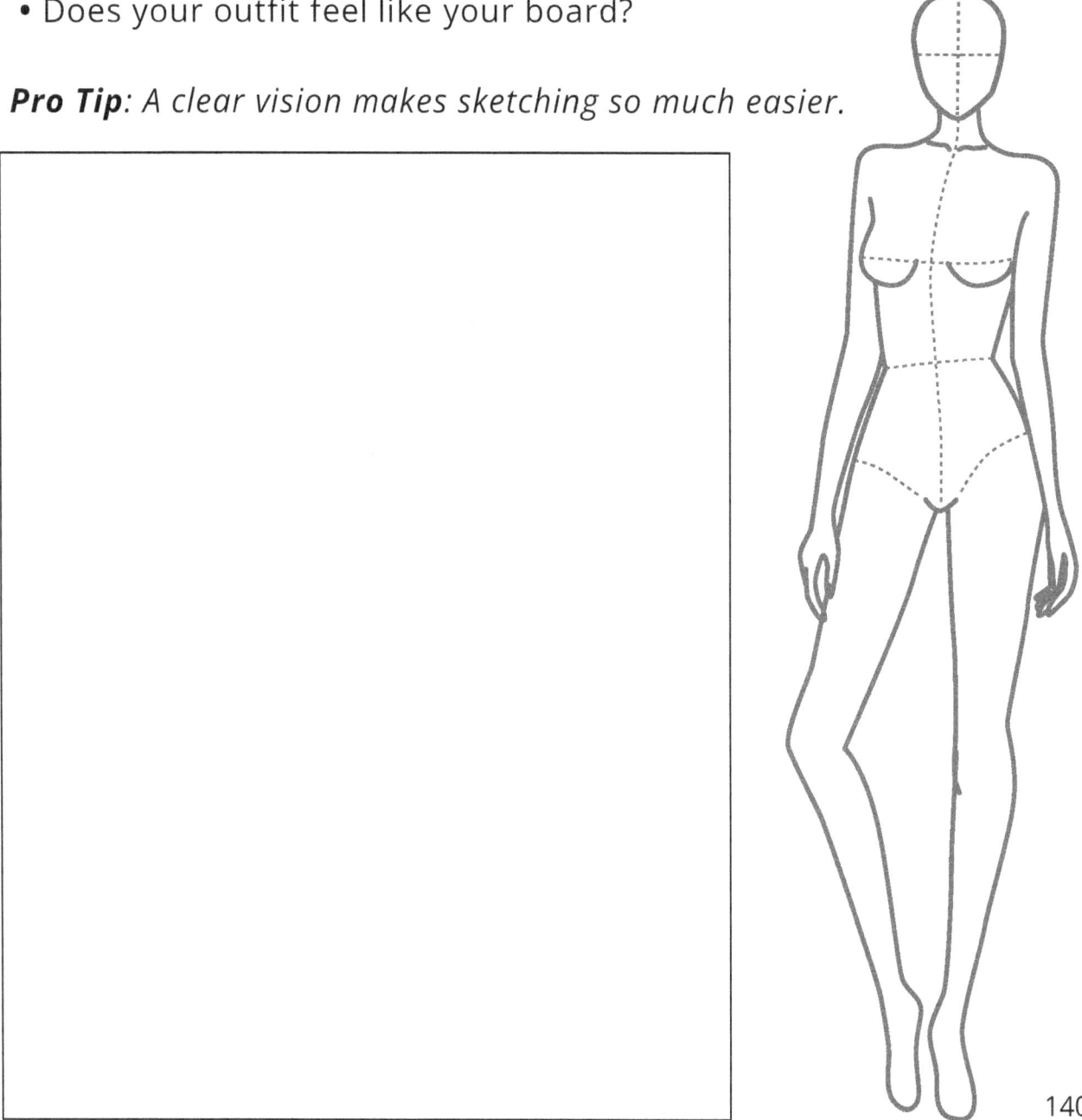

Designer Checklist for Teens

Everything you need for your creative sessions-check it off as you build your toolkit!

Sketching Essentials
- Sketchbooks & Paper ....
- Fashion Figure Templates ....
- Pencils (HB, 2B, 4B) ....
- Fine Liners & Ink Pens ....
- Erasers & Sharpeners ....
- Ruler / French Curves ....

Color Zone
- Colored Pencils / Markers ....
- Watercolors or Gouache ....
- Fabric Swatches / Texture Samples ....

Creative Tools
- Scissors / Glue / Tape ....
- Measuring Tape / Pins ....
- Mini Portfolio Folder ....

Digital Extras (Optional)
- Tablet + Stylus ....
- Drawing Apps or Fashion Design Software ....

Inspiration Sources
- Textile Catalogs / Magazines ....
- Moodboard Materials / Pinterest Clips ....

Pro Tip: Your tools are your superpowers-keep them ready.

My Favorite Fabrics & Brands
– Notes & Swatches

Write down the textures and materials you love most!

Add fabric snippets, tape swatches, or photos of favorite brands.

- Top 3 Fabrics I Love: ....
- Fabrics I Want to Try: ....
- Favorite Stores / Brands: ....
- Fabric That Matches My Style: ....
- Dream Material to Design With: ....

Pro Tip: *Your fabric choices tell your story as a designer.*

_____
_____
_____
_____
_____
_____
_____
_____
_____
_____

My Personal Fashion Journal

You've reached the final section-but it's really your beginning as a teen designer. Use this page to capture your creative thoughts and what you've learned.

- What I learned so far: ....
- My favorite designs: ....
- The style that feels most "me": ....
- My next goals as a designer: ....

Every sketch is a step forward - keep drawing, keep exploring, keep growing.

_____
_____
_____
_____
_____
_____
_____
_____
_____
_____

Congratulations! You Did It!

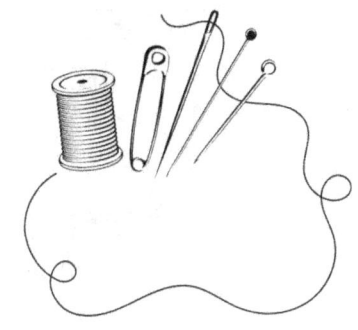

Congratulations, Designer!

You made it to the last section-amazing job! Every page you filled helped you grow your creativity, style, and confidence.

Fashion isn't just clothes; it's self-expression. Through every sketch, you've built a visual language that's uniquely you.

Keep in mind:
- Growth = Practice + Passion
- Your style is your superpower
- Never stop creating

We'd Love to Hear From You!

If this book inspired you, share your feedback or tag your designs online so others can join the journey.

   Pro Tip: *The world needs your vision-keep showing it!*

Niky Jadesson

Thank You!
(final message)

Thank You for Being Here!

We hope this teen sketchbook inspired you to design, explore, and dream big.

Your creativity means everything to us!

If you'd like to share ideas, thoughts, or suggestions, we'd love to hear from you:

 nikyjadesson@gmail.com

You can also find more creative sketchbooks by searching **Niky Jadesson Books** online.

Keep sketching, keep learning, and keep shining bright!

Thank You for Choosing This Book!

  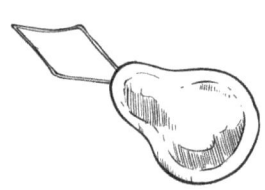 

We're so proud of the imagination and effort you've put into your designs.

If this book helped you grow your skills, leaving a short review really helps others discover it too.

Want More?
Search **Niky Jadesson Books** for more creative versions and design themes!

Remember:
- Keep sketching
- Keep designing
- Keep creating

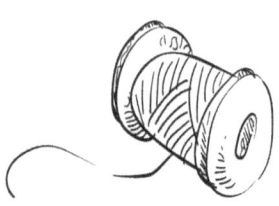

Niky Jadesson

About the Author

Niky Jadesson is an author and designer who believes learning should always be creative and fun.

Her books help young artists and dreamers explore fashion, art, and self-expression with confidence.

She finds inspiration in nature walks, coffee moments, and the endless curiosity that comes from sketching new ideas.

Her mission: to inspire the next generation of creators- one page at a time.

Discover more by searching **Niky Jadesson Books.**

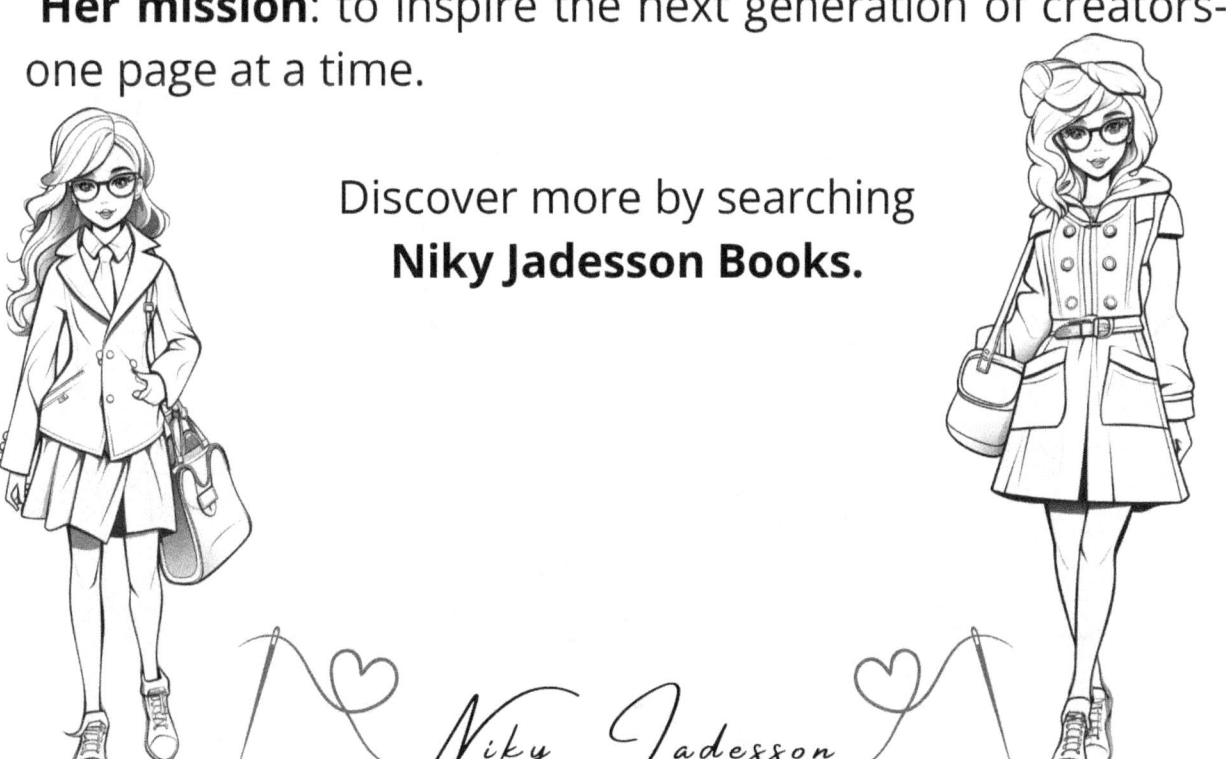

Mini Glossary of Fashion Terms (for Teens)

- **Silhouette** – The overall shape of a design.
- **Pattern** – Template used to cut fabric pieces.
- **Drape** – How a fabric falls or moves.
- **Seam** – The line where two fabrics join.
- **Hemline** – The bottom edge of a garment.
- **Bodice** – The upper body part of clothing.
- **Pleat** – A fold adding shape or movement.
- **Textile** – Any woven or knitted fabric.
- **Fiber** – What fabric is made from (cotton, silk, etc.).
- **Layering** – Styling by combining multiple garments.
- **Moodboard** – A collage of visuals for design inspiration.
- **Trend** – A popular style or color at the moment.
- **Sustainable Fashion** – Design that respects the planet.
- **Fast Fashion** – Trendy but quickly-made clothing.
- **Haute Couture** – Luxury, hand-made, one-of-a-kind designs.
- **Capsule Wardrobe** – A few pieces that mix & match perfectly.
- **Collection** – A group of coordinated designs by one creator.

Pro Tip: *Learning the language of fashion helps you design like a pro.*

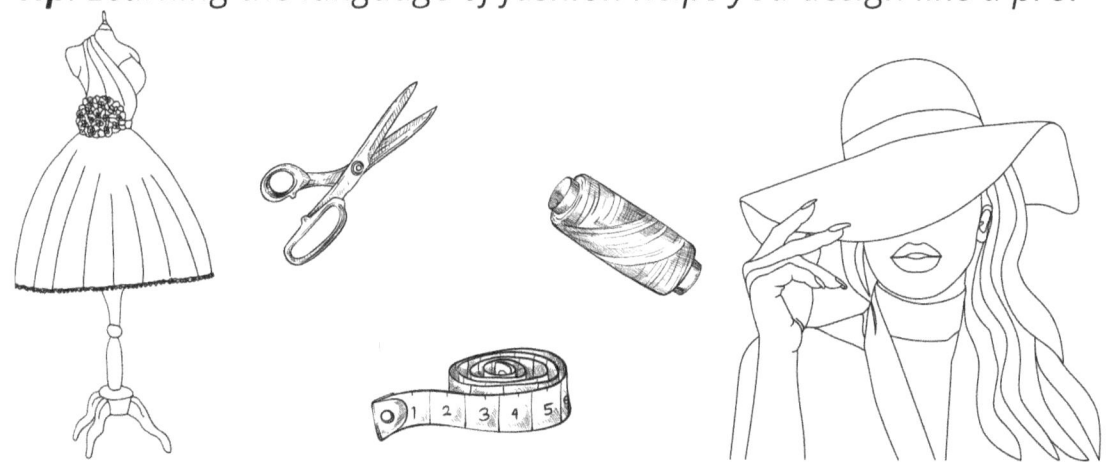

Certificate of Completion

FASHION DESIGN SKETCHBOOK – TEEN EDITION
by Niky Jadesson Books

This certifies that

_____

Has completed this **Fashion Design Sketchbook**
with creativity, imagination, and dedication!

You've explored trends, practiced figure drawing, experimented with textures, and developed your own fashion voice.

Every sketch you made is a step toward your artistic future.
Be proud! Stay inspired! Keep creating!

Signed: _____

(Your Signature)

Date: _____

Pro Tip: This isn't the end - it's your next beginning.
The world is ready for your designs!

www.ingramcontent.com/pod-product-compliance
Lightning Source LLC
Chambersburg PA
CBHW081359070526
44583CB00020B/2604